JEWS IN A FREE SOCIETY:
Challenges and Opportunities

JEWS IN A
FREE SOCIETY:
Challenges and
Opportunities

Edited by *Edward A. Goldman*

HEBREW UNION COLLEGE PRESS
1978

Library of Congress Cataloging in Publication Data
Main entry under title:

Jews in a free society.

1. Judaism—Addresses, essays, lectures. 2. Judaism—
United States—Addresses, essays, lectures. 3. Reform
Judaism—Addresses, essays, lectures. I. Goldman, Ed-
ward A., 1941-
BM40.J45   296   78-9753
ISBN 0-87820-112-2

MANUFACTURED IN THE UNITED STATES OF AMERICA

This publication is made possible through contributions to the Quinquennial Fund by members of the Hebrew Union College–Jewish Institute of Religion Rabbinic Alumni Association.

Contents

Preface

One hundred years is little time in the history of the Jews. Indeed, the Jewish awareness of their place in the long continuum of history bears with it the inevitable realization that Centennials represent only beginnings for Jewish institutions. Yet we merit pride in our beginnings, for the Hebrew Union College became the first permanent modern rabbinical seminary in America, and one hundred years later it is a great international institution of Jewish learning. Furthermore, one hundred years is a significant span of time in the life of these United States and in the life of the American Jewish community.

When the Centennial Committee began to consider appropriate ways to observe the one hundredth anniversary of the College, a consensus quickly emerged that the Cincinnati celebration should include one series of events which would feature the faculty doing that which they do best—teaching. The inspiration for this plan came from the great Babylonian Academy of Sura, which was founded by Rab in the year 219 c.e. Sura was a rabbinical school, and as such it had a permanent student body. However, twice a year, at the commencement of autumn (Elul) and spring (Adar), Jews from throughout Babylonia flocked to Sura to study the Law. This assembly was called the Kallah, and was made up of students diverse in age and in degree of academic attainment. The non-permanent disciples would prepare themselves for the Kallah-month during the prior five months, since at the end of the previous session the head of the Academy would announce the next treatise to be studied. And then they would convene, scholar and layman, to learn together and to affirm by their participation their commitment to Jewish learning. The Centennial Committee was inspired by this ancient example of adult education, and so, in the spirit of the Kallah, the Centennial Academy was conceived.

The Cincinnati School owes its very existence to the Jewish community of Cincinnati. A Cincinnati rabbi, Isaac Mayer Wise, founded it, and Jewish leaders from Cincinnati have continually served as dedicated supporters. Therefore, the Centennial Committee wanted to say thank you to Cincinnati for our one hundred years of fruitful co-existence by inviting the community to come and learn with us. Although the rich heritage of Jewish learning has always been preserved and nurtured primarily by a scholar class of rabbis and teachers, the scholars could not function without a community supportive of their goals. By inviting the Cincinnati community to share in our academic enterprise, we were again confirming the bond that links school to community.

The Centennial Academy Lectures continued for two months, each Tuesday night in October and November of 1975. The overall topic for the Academy was "Jews in a Free Society: Challenges and Opportunites." The convergence of the College Centennial and the national Bicentennial provided a unique occasion to assess the interrelationship between America and American Jewry. Therefore, each Academy Lecturer was asked by the Centennial Committee to apply the insights of his own discipline to the situation of contemporary Jews in America, elucidating both the challenges and the opportunities. The lectures herein printed deal with the American Jewish Experience: the history, the sociology, the artistic creativity, and the ways in which the ancient legacy of religious ideas and literature can thrive in a free democracy.

These lectures were, of course, written for spoken delivery, and clearly, an oral presentation may differ stylistically and in impact from a written academic and literary document. For instance, one of the lectures, that of David Weisberg, was accompanied with slides. But the Committee decided to entrust the lectures to print because of the overwhelming reception from the Cincinnati community, and out of a conviction that others would enjoy participating in the Academy in absentia.

Thanks are due to the many people who made the Centennial Academy Lectures possible. The Centennial Committee was chaired by Samuel Sandmel, and the members were Chanan Brichto, Edward Goldman, Robert Katz, Eugene Mihaly, and Ellis Rivkin, with John Friedman serving as student liaison to the Committee. Vera Sanker was Centennial Coordinator and Docent Chairperson. The other Docents who worked on behalf of the lectures were Helen Benjamin, Cecelia Berman, Marilynn Braude, Carolyn Dunkelman, Jane Ellis, Pegge Garfield, Flo Hersch, Ellen Kleinfeld, Marcia Lowenstein, Elly Miller, Pat Passer, Letty Rabiner, Irene Schwartz, Ruth Schwartz, Mary Ethel Sharon, and Nancy Hornbach. A special debt of gratitude is owed to Ruth Frenkel and her staff, who arranged beautiful receptions following each lecture.

We also owe thanks to those members of the Cincinnati Committee for the Centennial Celebration who presented the lecturers. The Chairman of the Committee, Justin Friedman, introduced President Alfred Gottschalk. The others who introduced speakers were Judge Gilbert Bettman, Dr. Stanley Block, Philip T. Cohen, Melville Dunkelman, David Joseph, Melvin Korelitz, David Lazarus, Philip Meyers, Jr., Gary Rabiner, Myron Rudd, Dr. Edward Saeks, Dr. Leon Silverman, Charles Tobias, and the late Simon Lazarus, Jr.

Once again, we are deeply indebted to the Cincinnati community. Their enthusiastic and dedicated support of the Centennial Academy brought forth the idea for this book.

EDWARD A. GOLDMAN

The Public Function of the Jewish Scholar

An Introduction

ALFRED GOTTSCHALK

In 1832, Leopold Zunz, the founder of *Wissenschaft des Judentums*, the discipline dealing with the scholarly exploration of Judaism in all its historical and literary aspects, published *Die gottesdienstlichen Vortraege der Juden* (The Synagogal Lectures of the Jews). This is the book of which the noted church historian August Friedrich Gfroerer, the author's contemporary, said that it was the greatest contribution to knowledge made by a Jew since the time of Spinoza. The work explained the nature and history of the Jewish sermon. It also commented on the religious and intellectual condition of the Jews in Zunz's day, pleaded for the renewal and propagation of *wissenschaftliche Cultur* among the Jews, and lamented the absence of learned institutions and professors who could engage in developing and spreading such *Cultur*.

Cultur is a German word which, like another German word of related meaning, namely *Bildung*, is difficult to translate. The term *Cultur* touches many meanings and reaches into many layers of man's creative activities. I translate it as "culture"—being aware of the

Dr. Alfred Gottschalk is President of Hebrew Union College–Jewish Institute of Religion and Professor of Bible and Jewish Religious Thought.

definition by Preserved Smith, who understood by culture "that complex whole that includes knowledge, belief, morals, law, customs, opinions, religion and art." So long as we are cognizant of that wide range we know what Zunz meant by *wissenschaftliche Cultur:* culture in the above sense legitimatized by scholarly research.

It took decades until Zunz's call for appropriate institutions of higher Jewish learning was heeded. In 1854 the Jewish Theological Seminary was founded in Breslau, Germany; the Hochschule fuer die Wissenschaft des Judentums opened in Berlin in 1872; and our own Hebrew Union College in Cincinnati in 1875. In a way they all accepted the scientific method which Zunz had expounded since its inception. At the same time, however, all of them, and other similar institutions that followed, narrowed Zunz's concept. While Zunz and his friends, in the early days of *Wissenschaft des Judentums,* had reached out for the fullness of modern Jewish cultural life derived from and refined by scholarly findings, the later nineteenth-century Jewish scholars contracted that concept and concentrated on theology, history, and philology. While the younger Zunz saw in Jewish scholarship an instrument helpful to vital contemporary Jewish life, his successors too often saw Jewish scholarship as an end in itself. In fact, one of them, the great Moritz Steinschneider (1816–1907), historian of Jewish literature and Semitica bibliographer sans pareil, looking in bitter disappointment at the Jewry of his time, regarded his life's work merely as the means to provide a decent funeral for the remnants of Judaism.

What gives cause to these historical remarks is the publication in this volume of the lectures which the faculty of our Cincinnati School presented to the larger community during the College's Centennial Year. Through these lectures Jewish scholars attempted the propagation, to repeat Zunz's term, of Jewish *wissenschaftliche Cultur,* the spreading of Jewish information filtered through the channels of critical Jewish learning, discussion of contemporary problems and concerns in the light of scholarly findings. The very nature of these lectures, lectures by scholars moving out of the strict confines of their specialty and addressing not students and scholars but a Jewish lay audience at large, presents a welcome opportunity to discuss the *public* function of the Jewish scholar.

That the Jewish scholar has such a function is a fact that was not always noted, and if noted not always approved. There appear to be two main reasons for this neglect. The first concerns a long-lasting attitude of the American institutions of higher learning, colleges as well as universities. Generally speaking, although there were a small number of exceptions prior to World War I, the majority of American academic institutions followed strong pragmatic trends in determining their aims and methods. One need merely read Abraham Flexner's critical writings on American colleges and graduate schools, published between 1908 and 1930, to realize how overwhelmingly strong the tendency was toward training for practical skills and "trade school" abilities. Flexner's investigations pointed out how deep the gap was between English and German academe on the one hand and American on the other. Clearly, the latter, mostly for reasons of long-standing and only slowly receding ideology, was little inclined to involve the American university in the affairs of the community or the world. It is interesting that the rabbinic seminaries of America, Hebrew Union College as well as Jewish Theological Seminary, followed European standards and norms long before they became common for the majority of American institutions of higher learning. The reason was simple enough. Their academic leadership and faculties were products of European universities. However, at the same time this meant that their academic behavior and instincts were unduly ivory-towerish; their separation from the Jewish populace was more pronounced than one would have expected.

There is a second reason which for a period of time kept minimal, or made unnecessary, the public function of the Jewish professor. America's Jewish history is a history of immigrants. The main task of American Jewry, as long as new immigrants entered in massive waves, was the social integration of these Jewish masses into the American body politic and body cultural. The problems of the Jewish immigrant were seen as preponderantly educational, social, and eco-nomic—all of them secular concerns of which schools, social centers, and the labor movement would take care. In that respect it is sympto-matic that some of the personalities who were active in the founding and shaping of the Jewish Theological Seminary were inclined to regard it as an instrumentality serving, in the last end, the Americanization of the East European immigrant. The survival of Judaism and Jewishness in America had not become a problem yet. Each new wave of immigrants provided a fresh infusion of Jewish vitality, and although a good deal of Jewish substance was lost as Jews adjusted to the new world, the loss for a considerable time was made up by the arrival of new immigrants.

But then mass immigration stopped. The adjustment of the Jewish immigrant to the American scene was more or less complete, and the progressive integration of the Jew into the American scene brought with it all the well-known phenomena of de-Judaization, namely, alienation from the synagogue, the loss in conscious Jewish religiosity resulting in the weakening or giving up of religious home practice, the thinning of Jewish loyalties, illiteracy in matters Jewish, mixed marriage, etc. There were counter forces—the Nazi persecution of Jews and the Holocaust, the founding of the State of Israel and the threats to her existence—which resulted in the need for American Jewry to involve itself as a group in the affairs of world Jewry. However, this "new" manner of being a Jew substantially differed from the individual and group Jewishness of American Jewry of earlier generations. Elements of cohesion which had been eminently effective, such as landsmanschaften and family tradition, had weakened and were disappearing. American Jewry increasingly submitted to voluntarism in joining synagogues and Jewish organizations. This voluntarism was accompanied by strong motivations for Jewish identification. Yet, it was basically different from the Jewishness that the immigrant had brought with him. The new Jewishness required justification and articulation—and constant reaffirmation. Too often an emotional reaction to Jewish distress, it required fortification of more permanent character. Charged with Jewish energy by the emergencies of successive Jewish world crises, it needed a lasting foundation built on Jewish ideas carrying conviction.

The answer to this need was a new concept of Jewish education. Expanded beyond the classroom of the religious school and the halls of the synagogue, the scope and meaning of Jewish education widened. Jewish education in a broad sense leading to "Jewish literacy" possessed by every Jew is seen today as one of the main answers, perhaps even the essential answer, to the problem of making Judaism survive as a vibrant power and a live source of Jewish identity, conviction, loyalty, and activity.

In this situation an institution of higher Jewish learning like ours finds one of its main challenges. A college devoted to Jewish learning is a natural source and center for the kind of Jewish education that is demanded today. Indeed, Hebrew Union College–Jewish Institute of Religion has engaged in "outreach programs" for some time and has continually intensified and widened them. Reaching out to the Jewish community has been our systematic aim for years. The effort of bringing the resources, the talents, and the services of the College-Institute to the large Jewish community outside our campuses has been markedly intensified by our Centennial enterprise. The faculty lectures of the Cincinnati School are a telling example of this intensification besides other programs carried out on the College-Institute's other campuses.

Educational outreach programs are not limited to Jewish institutions and Jewish audiences. The general American colleges and universities, as they emancipated themselves from their origins and early traditions as training and trade schools, assumed an educational responsibility to the larger non-academic community, very often an obligation to all members of the family of man. It is interesting to note that this course somewhat coincided with the retreat of American political isolationism and the emergence of the United States as a world power. One cannot illustrate the incisive change better than by quoting from older books, pamphlets, and speeches, produced in the Anglo-Saxon world, that deal with the meaning and the uses of higher learning and its institutions. T. H. Huxley, in the nineties of the last century, saw the meaning of the modern university in the fact that while the medieval university looked backwards and professed to be a storehouse of old knowledge, the modern university was looking forward, being a factory of new knowledge. To Thomas Carlyle, fifty years earlier, the true university was a collection of books. John Henry Newman, in 1852, defined the university as a place of instruction where universal knowledge is professed. And to conclude with the heretical statement of an Ivy League president, Woodrow Wilson, speaking in Pittsburgh in 1914, said, "The use of a university is to make young gentlemen as unlike their fathers as possible."

Obviously, none of these statements would do today. Quoting Kenneth W. Thompson, "we have linked education to the open society." Colleges and universities are active agents in that society. The professors do no longer live in a secluded cloister. Each one, potentially at least, is an *homme engagé,* a man of affairs even if he is a thinker, in fact, just because he is a thinker.

The faculty lectures published in this volume greatly differ from one another. But taken altogether, they represent fine examples of the professor fulfilling a public function by moving out of the curricular classroom into the public area. By linking the scholarly interests to broader Jewish interests and discussion, the professor does not become an intruder into foreign territory. The community of intelligent adults, Jewish and other, seeks the service of the learned man for successful application of new knowledge to its affairs. It makes sense to speak again of "the mission of the scholar," to quote a term (*Die Bestimmung des Gelehrten*) coined by the philosopher Johann Gottlieb Fichte (1762–1814), who was not only a follower of Kant, building philosophical systems, but also an educator introducing new concepts of university education. Jews today have come to recognize that mission. It is extremely gratifying that a steadily increasing number of congregations invites our professors to spend time in their communities as "scholars in residence."

In his public function the scholar faces an audience exposed to the Jewish tremors of our time. His mission is to help form a durable Jewish *weltbild* and provide values, norms, and insights which are useful in clarifying issues. Some of the professors who have served in such public capacity have reported that the community expected of them help in making a choice between conflicting ideas. I do not think this is the task of a professor, and I do not think this is the task of the College. The trouble with many of our Jewish discussions is their poverty of ideas. Our public arguments too often lack clear-cut notions and the possibility of choice between ideas. Most frequently it appears that the present Jewish scene is characterized by conflicting emotions rather than conflicting ideas. Quoting Kenneth W. Thompson once more, "The educated man . . . is someone not locked in by passions. He is sensitive to alternatives and aware of consequences." Toward that aim the education of the Jewish public should strive. Public Jewish opinion, now often more distinguished by its intent and climate than by its contents, should be based on ideas. Jewish policy, shaped by a wide spectrum of moods, recollections, passions, slogans, and cliches, should be examined rationally. Emotional arguments should be probed intellectually and thus made more secure. We must demonstrate the danger of words and moods so inflated that their intrinsic value as well as their potential for intelligent communication is greatly diminished.

In his public function the professor's primary charge is to act as the intellectual conscience which carefully examines and carefully argues without being swayed by undisciplined emotion. For all of this the Jewish scholar must have the support of his school. The College must back its faculty's public service with a corresponding attitude of service, with a general scholarly point of view, and with a sense of mission. True, the Jewish professor speaks for himself; he is not a mouthpiece for a collective. Yet, his public function is best achieved if it is apparent that he belongs to a learned body which has succeeded in maintaining a high measure of Jewish unity while at the same time maintaining the right to ideological diversity. In this manner, the professor's intellectual contribution acquires and retains a most convincing stance and reveals a Jewish life style built on the kind of intellectual and religious conviction which is gained from careful and free choice.

Genesis: College Beginnings

JACOB R. MARCUS

We're here for a birthday party. Our College was a hundred years old this week. We were born on October 4, 1875. That's apparently a long time ago, but if you think in biblical terms, it doesn't mean a thing, because Methuselah lived to be almost a thousand years of age; so, you see, we've just really started our career.

Some of you might ask this question: Why did we have to have a college in the first place? Why did they start a school? And to understand that, we have to go back a bit. We know why Harvard started. It started in 1636 because the Puritans wanted a learned ministry. That, too, was part of our problem in the decades before the Civil War. We not only wanted a learned ministry; we wanted a respectable ministry.

Some of you may say to me, "Just what do you mean by that word 'respectable'? Just what happened in the past?" Well, I'm thinking of a friend of mine who lived in the 1840s, a man named "Roley" Marks. Roley was a nickname. Actually, his name was Albert J. Marks. He made a living as an actor and he was also a part-time

Dr. Jacob R. Marcus is Milton and Hattie Kutz Distinguished Service Professor of American Jewish History, Director of the American Jewish Archives and American Jewish Periodical Center.

rabbi. He was more or less a full-time fireman, also, with a volunteer fire company, and when he heard that bell ring, he left the pulpit, ran and grabbed his coat and hat, and joined his company. When reproached, he always had a good argument. His argument was that God could take care of himself, but the burning building could not.

I have often suspected, also, that he not only worshipped at the altar of Judaism but also at the altar of John Barleycorn. At all events, on one Rosh Hashanah Eve in the 1840s, he preached and he didn't do so well. Maybe he wasn't altogether there, and he was reproached by some people who were present. This angered him very very much. The following morning he rose and instead of preaching indulged in a tirade against his critics; his climactic phrase was, "Jesus Christ, who says I'm not a rabbi?"

Conditions like that continued for quite a long time. Early in the twentieth century, Beaumont, Texas, advertised for a rabbi. They wanted a man who could get along socially with everybody; a man who was a good mixer; and after their advertisement appeared Jewish editors began to comment: "What Beaumont wants is not a rabbi but a bartender."

The man who realized what this country needed was Isaac Mayer Wise. He was a Bohemian who came to these shores in 1846; an exceedingly attractive young man, a charming fellow, a beautiful person.

Wise was a rebel. In his day there was a law in Bohemia called the *Matrikel Gesetz*. Rabbis could only marry one person in the family because the government didn't want the Jews to propagate. They wanted to "kill them off." Wise paid no attention to laws; he got in trouble with the authorities and finally decided to come to America where he could develop and do what he wanted to do.

He was more or less a stormy petrel. He was always in trouble; got himself an Orthodox congregation, 1846, Albany, and soon became a religious radical. He did things no respectable Orthodox Jew would do. He would write on the Sabbath. He would swing in a swing on a holiday. That's all work. You're not supposed to do those things. And he had ideas, newfangled ideas about art music. In those days not only the Orthodox Jews looked askance at art music, but so did some of the Christians, people whom we today would call

Fundamentalists. Wise himself tells of an incident in a church, no doubt in Albany, where instrumental music was forbidden, and where a choir leader had smuggled a little two-pronged tuning fork into the choir loft and had used it to get the pitch. When a deacon noticed this he stood up in the congregation and yelled at the choir leader in a stentorian tone: "Take that instrument of Hell out of this house of God," and that tuning fork had to be removed.

Wise made one terrible mistake. He fought with the president of his congregation. That's always a mistake, for the president got his cronies together and they fired Isaac Mayer Wise shortly before Rosh Hashanah 1850, but the rabbi refused to stay fired. He knew he had the congregation with him, so when Rosh Hashanah morning came, and he went up to the pulpit to perform the services, the president took a poke at him. If I know Isaac Mayer Wise, he poked him back. I have always maintained that those were the blows that were heard around the world. In a way that was the beginning of organized Reform Judaism. Wise seceded the following day with his friends and established a Reform congregation. Eight years after he had come to this country he was such a notable leader that Cincinnati's Bene Yeshurun Congregation invited him to come down here to be their rabbi. What's important about this is that—with the possible exception of New Orleans—Cincinnati was the largest community between the Allegheny and the Pacific Coast, the Pacific Ocean. So here was a man who was catapulted almost immediately into a tremendously big and important job.

That was in 1854. In 1866 he built that magnificent cathedral downtown which we call the Isaac Mayer Wise Temple. It was in that decade of the 1860s that something happened which was to have a tremendous impact upon American life and upon American Jewish life. A group of capitalists got together in an obscure little village in the Rocky Mountains in the Territory of Utah at a place called Promontory Point. There, one man reached into his pocket and pulled out a golden spike. Another had a silver sledgehammer; and they drove that golden spike into an oak tie and by that symbolic act they completed the first transcontinental American railroad. The Atlantic and Pacific were now united, and a land that had been through four years of Civil War and had been cemented in blood was now reinforced by bands of steel. More important, space and time were annihilated. People could move anywhere in a hurry; and it was then that Isaac Mayer Wise decided there was a need to unite all of the Jewish congregations here in the United States.

He had the complete support of a group of enlightened lay people here in Cincinnati. Without them he could not have done anything. They helped him; they advised him; they supplied the money; and so they organized a union of American Jewish congregations, but did not call it a union of Jewish congregations because the word "Jew" in those days was a dirty word even for Jews. Much more respectable was the term "Hebrew"; so they named it the Union of American Hebrew Congregations.

That was in 1873. The prime purpose of the Union was to create a college to train American rabbis in the American spirit, respectable rabbis and learned rabbis. That was its job; and so they created a seminary. It was not a Reform college; that was made perfectly clear. The word "Reform" or "Liberal" does not occur anywhere in the early literature. It was a school to unite all the Jews of America. They needed unity; so it was to be a Union College, but they couldn't call it a Union College because there were several Christian Union Colleges in the country, so it was to be called a Jewish Union College, but inasmuch as Jews refused to call it a Jewish Union College, it had to be a Hebrew Union College, and thus on October 4, 1875 they held their first session in the cellar, the vestry rooms of the Mound Street Temple. They had about ten young folk, teenagers, when they opened the doors. Shortly after they opened they got a recruit, a girl. She wasn't a teenager. She was in the seventh grade of the public school, and she was eleven years of age. She should have been home sitting on the kitchen floor juggling jacks instead of juggling Hebrew irregular verbs.

They also had a library. What's a college without a library? And they locked the library up every night in a two-and-a-half-foot wooden box, and they locked it up not because they were afraid the youngsters would go off and steal the books, but they were afraid down there on Mound Street that the mice would come out of the panels and eat the books.

A few years later they were so successful—they really were successful—that they bought an elegant mansion down on West Sixth Street, not too far from Baymiller, and they opened it in 1881, and I went to that school the last year that they kept it open. By this time the library had really grown tremendously and they had bookcases in almost every room in the building. Of course the boys busted the panes in the bookcases, but I found that very convenient because when I came to my classes, which started at 3:00 o'clock, I would simply saunter into what Dr. Kaufmann Kohler used to call the "lunching room"—he meant the lounging room, of course—and I would prop up my chair against one of the broken bookcases, and I knew which one I liked; I wouldn't even look; I'd reach back and take out a volume, one of the six volumes of Graetz's *History of the Jews,* and I would read as I would a dime novel, and that was the beginning of an American Jewish historian.

Those of you who know these old houses, and some of you do know them, know that the third floors were usually very large and spacious, and they were used as dancing rooms. You could have a reception there, but the College didn't use the third floor as a dancing hall; it used it as a chapel, and they put in pews there, and occasionally Bernard Bettmann would come and would talk to the boys. He was the chairman of the Board from 1875 on till well into the twentieth century. He was a fine gentleman, a very cultured gentleman. He had a slight German accent and spoke with a heavy guttural intonation, and it wasn't in my time—possibly a year or so before me, so it was told me—that he had come to school and addressed the boys, telling them all to go out and dissimulate Judaism, and they took his advice and have been doing it ever since.

Now, you may be surprised by the fact that the first students were very young. They were very few and they were very young. Don't be surprised at the paucity of the numbers. The typical American academy or college of the seventeenth, eighteenth, and ninetenth centuries had but a handful of students. As a matter of fact, when Oliver Wendell Holmes wrote a poem celebrating the bicentennial of Harvard in 1836, two hundred years after it opened, this is what he said:

> And who was on the Catalogue
> When College was begun?

Two nephews of the President,
And *the* Professor's son. . . .
Lord' how the seniors knocked about
The freshman class of one!

So it wasn't unusual to have such a small number of students and such young ones.

We were in no hurry to graduate. We were young and willing to wait. The College, after a few years, became a nine-year school. You went four years to high school; you went four years to the university; and then, because we were getting along in a scholastic sense, you enjoyed one year of graduate work.

We boys all lived in Avondale or Walnut Hills, and we used to walk down from those suburbs all the way to the school, about two miles or more. My classmate who is, thank God, still living, Abe Shinedling, when he had his shoes soled, used to put on two soles because he not only walked down from the hills to near Baymiller but walked all the way back after school was over. We were so poor we couldn't afford the nickel for the car ride, so we walked to high school. We went to Woodward High School downtown near Liberty. Then at 2:15, when we were let out, we ran to make our 3:00 class, and we stayed at the school from 3:00 to 6:00, and then like princes, we would spend a nickel, and we would take the streetcar back home.

Now, you must understand that most of us were about fifteen or sixteen. We worked very hard, twenty-five hours a week at least at high school, fifteen hours at the College; and of course we got tired and we got bored. Occasionally we were unhappy; and because we had high spirits and were full of beans, we sometimes cut up a bit.

Before my time they had a German-born professor who was rather naive, and the boys would play the same trick on him often. During the winter season they would take some snow and mold it into a hard ice ball and put it under the gas jet; and when, after awhile, that snow began to melt, the Herr Professor would turn solemnly to his class and say, "Boys, the gas is leaking."

We had other forms of divertissement. What we would do is this: The smallest among us, and some were only in kneepants, would crawl under the batwing doors of the toilets and lock them from the inside. At 5:00 the faculty would rush down—they were a bunch of elderly men—and would frantically start to push at those doors writhing in agony. There are some people who maintain that this was the beginning of the Charleston dance. That's all wrong. It was the Virginia reel.

My favorite professor—and we all liked him—was Dr. Jacob Z. Lauterbach. The Doctor frequently had the 5:00 to 6:00 hour, and we liked him because he was a voracious eater, and we knew that when he got hungry he would always let us out a little bit early. When we moved up here on the hill and we finally had a dormitory, he was the man who was always called upon to recite the blessing over the bread and the wine on a Friday night, the *kiddush*. One Friday night he wasn't there, and he was always the first man at the table. The boys knew something was wrong. They looked around, and they finally found him outside the door of the dormitory. He was talking to a black cat on this Friday night and he was saying, "Shoo, cat; go way cat; go way cat," but the cat wouldn't go away, so the boys helped him in his misery. They drove the cat away, and he rushed in, hurried through the prayers, and after he had dug into the food and finished, the boys turned to him and they said, "Dr. Lauterbach, you are a distinguished Talmudist, you're a folklorist, a cultural anthropologist of note. How could you possibly believe such a superstition?" He looked at them quizzically, and in his heavy Austrian accent he said, "I'm modern and I'm scientific, but vy takes chences."

In 1912 we moved up here on the hill. The grounds had not been finished. They were still full of knolls and hummocks. We boys were recruited, got pick and shovel, and we had to level off the place. We made a nice ballfield. Most of the buildings we have today weren't standing then, and because there were so many hills here—and the hills were as high as those across at Burnet Woods—the catalogue of the College always said quite correctly, "The College is built on a bluff."

That wasn't true. The College was not built on a bluff. We boys had to work hard. You had to make a ninety-four average to get a scholarship or you were out of luck; and bear in mind you never carried less than thirty hours, fifteen at the university and fifteen at the College. The presidents of the school maintained the highest standards. There were Kohler, Morgenstern, Glueck, succeeded by our friend, the president of today, Dr. Alfred Gottschalk, who is driving us as we have been driven in the past, demanding that we do the best we can to maintain the high scholastic standards that have always distinguished the College.

When I went to the University of Berlin in 1922 to do graduate work and to get my doctorate, they refused to give me any credit for my University of Cincinnati studies. Of course, that was arrogant. The University wasn't that bad. It was a good school, and I was very happy there, but the Rector in Berlin would not give me a single credit for my work at the local university. They did give me all the credits I needed for the classes I had taken at the Hebrew Union College. Our school had a good name in Germany.

Although the students were young, many were exceptionally able. In the first class I taught, in 1920, I had a student who was so small he was still in kneepants; his feet would not reach the floor. His name was Joshua Loth Liebman. He graduated from the school and wrote a book called *Peace of Mind* that sold over a million copies.

Well what did the school actually do during the last hundred years? What did it accomplish. What did it teach? It has always had a point of view all its own. We are a liberal school. Theologically, we're unitarian. We believe that God created the world and that there is but one God. We believe, since God is the father of everyone, that every human being—man, woman, or child—is our brother, is a member of our common human family; we have no prejudice against anybody or against any religion, and that is why we are sympathetic to all religions and certainly sympathetic to Christianity.

Well, you may say to me, "That's a very liberal point of view, but you must have some body of knowledge, some body of theology. You must have something specific in which you believe. You must believe in revelation." Yes, we believe in revelation. We believe in the Ten Commandments, which were given to our fathers three thousand years ago. We think it's a magnificent code and a fine body of ethics. We do not believe, however, that the first and the last word was said at Mount Sinai. We believe that every new generation has its Mount Sinai, and every age produces its own Ten Commandments, that every generation has something new and beautiful to offer to us, and we reach out everywhere, to Christianity, to Islam, to any faith or to any good book or any beautiful picture, and take what we find beautiful and exalting and use it to enrich ourselves. We have our rituals; we have our ceremonies and we love them, but we have always maintained that the moral law is far more important than the ritual law.

Some of you may ask me, "Does Reform have a hierarchy? Does it have authority; isn't there somebody who can say go and somebody who can say stay?" No, we have no fixed authority. The only voice we recognize is the consensus, the ethical consensus of every generation. The only voice to which we listen is that which lies within us. Well, you may say to me, "If that's true, and there are 5,800,000 Jews in the United States, then there are 5,800,000 Judaisms in the United States," and my answer is, yes, thank God. Every man has his own faith and he lives by that faith.

We believe in science; and if there is anything in our past beliefs that is not congruent with the facts of science, then we revalue yesterday's rabbinic and religious traditions. Because we are modern and because we accept the findings of science, we are willing to divorce ourselves from some of the prejudices of the past, particularly where women are concerned. We have granted women a larger part in our synagogues and in our religious practices. We look upon them as equals. There have been women presidents of congregations for at least a generation. We have just graduated some women in our seminary, and we are determined to continue the policy of according them complete and absolute equality.

We do not believe in the physical resurrection. We do believe in some form of immortality. We do not believe in the concept of a personal Messiah, that some individual, a monarch, a member of the House of David, will yet appear, rule over us, and tell us what to do. That we completely reject. Though we do not accept the concept of a personal Messiah, we do believe in a Messianic age. We hope and pray and work for social justice. We strive to improve this world to the end that the masses, hundreds of thousands and millions in this country and abroad, may not remain ill-fed and ill-clothed, and ill-housed.

What has Reform to do with the ushering in of the Messianic age? We believe we have a mission to perform. It is our job to help bring it about. Does that mean that we Jews believe that we are *the* Chosen People? Certainly not. We reject that concept, yet we believe that every people in a way is a chosen people. Every people believes it has something to say, a job to do, and we believe it has been our obligation, since the days of the prophets, to preach social justice, righteousness, decency, opportunity for every human being, black and white, Jew and Gentile. This is our job. That is the mission that we have to perform; and because we have that task, that goal, we believe that we can perform it wherever we are. A generation ago, Reform maintained that the only place you could have fulfilled that mission was in the land where you lived and where you wanted to be. There was no need to go back to Palestine, and for that reason many of our leaders of yesterday were anti-Zionists, strongly anti-Zionistic.

Today we have a better understanding. We believe that a man can be a good friend of Israel, do everything he possibly can to help our fellow Jews in the Holy Land live their lives to the fullest, and at the same time we, wherever we are, work as human beings to make this world a better place for everyone. And because we live in this world and affirm it and its positive values with vigor, we have embraced education. We are passionate partisans of the arts and sciences. It is no accident, therefore, that the Jews of the United States, with less than 3 percent of the population, have won at least 15 percent of all the Nobel Prizes in the physical sciences.

We are—you'll excuse me for saying it—a successful religious group. This may shock you or surprise you, but it is true. We are the largest liberal religious movement in the world. We have grown internationally. There is no continent where you will not find graduates of the Hebrew Union College. You'll find them in Australia, South Africa, South America, Canada, and I like to parody the statement that was made about the British Empire: the sun never sets on a graduate of the Hebrew Union College, and pray God that sun never will set.

Thus endeth the first book, the Book of Genesis, after a hundred years. I do hope that all of you come back here at the end of the next hundred years and permit me to review that new century.

The Advantages of Being an Ancient People

SAMUEL GREENGUS

When I was a little boy and first became aware of being Jewish, I was surprised to discover how much there was for me to learn. There was the task of learning to read Hebrew so I could recite my prayers. I can still remember the exotic and mysterious black letters, printed large and full, making a rhythmic pattern across the white pages of the prayer book. It was not long before I could read; and I was praised by my parents and teachers for reading rapidly and fluently; this was necessary because there were many pages of prayers to read and recite.

But reading was not enough. I soon discovered that there was more for me to study. It was necessary to learn about the past; for all the important events of Jewish history seemed to have taken place before I was born. There were centuries of past history along with long shelves of venerable holy books that chronicled the past and that recorded the important teachings of my faith. I realized that if I ever hoped to become fully aware of what Judaism was all about, it would be necessary for me to spend many years of study, looking backwards into this past.

Dr. Samuel Greengus is Professor of Semitic Languages.

In retrospect, I see that I took to my Hebrew studies very well; I had a natural curiosity to know more about how things got to be the way they were. Then too, I lived near the Oriental Institute Museum of the University of Chicago; on weekends and during the summertime, I would visit and revisit the displays of ancient artifacts from Egypt, Babylonia, Persia, Canaan, and ancient Israel. From this combination of interests, I developed into a serious student, bent on exploring the past history and development of the Jewish people along with the general history of civilized man in the ancient Near East.

Studying is often hard work; when I was younger, I would at times wonder why it was necessary to work so hard in order to learn about my religion. Wouldn't it be nice to have all of the religious awareness I needed instantly—at one time—to be flooded with knowledge about God and the universe, about life and creation, to arrive at satisfactory answers without having to devote hours to reading, reflection, and evaluation?

But as I get older, I realize that true understanding only comes slowly, through trial and experience. This is true of life, and I believe that it is true for knowledge and religious understanding. Age and antiquity lend perspective; there are advantages to having a history and being able to look back on it. It is great to have sudden insights and flashes of ideas, but time remains the best test for ideas. We have to see if today's ideas will remain valid and attractive for tomorrow's thinkers. In the same way, with the help of history's perspective, we can test yesterday's ideas and see if they are valid for us today.

Tonight I want to explore with you some of the areas where this perspective of history has given us new awareness about the development of Jewish ideas. These are the advantages that come from being an ancient people.

Jewish identity, of course, consists of more than ideas; there are, as I see it, three components of Judaism: the ethnic, the political, and the religious. The ethnic is our sense of belonging to one people; it is a feeling that has grown out of the ancient tribal and kinship experience. All Jews believe themselves to be descended from Abraham and subsequently from one of the twelve tribes of Israel; and we view the non-Jew who becomes Jewish as becoming adopted into the family of Israel. Ethnic identity does not involve many conscious ideas; it is for most of us an accident of birth, a "gut" or visceral feeling of belonging to a kinship network beginning with our immediate family and extending outwards to all other Jews.

Another element is the political or national: this aspect of Jewish identity has come very much to the fore during the past decades and has blossomed with the rebirth of a Jewish state in Israel. For many Jews, nationality is an alternative to or replacement for religious identity. Some Jews simply see it as an extension of their ethnicity or kinship, while others view the state as a place where they can have fuller and freer expression for their religious practices. Nationhood is an ancient concept, going back to the Bible; but nationhood, like ethnicity, does not generate a great many conscious Jewish ideas. Jewish nationhood, is rather, a facilitator for the expression of Jewish ideas; it is not the end-product but a choice environment wherein Jewish experience can flourish.

The main source of Jewish ideas is the religious component. In my opinion, it is the central body which supports and gives life to the other strands of ethnicity and nationality. Without some sense of religious purpose, Jewish ethnicity and nationhood lose their uniqueness. Ethnicity and nationhood merge the individual into the context of a group. The religious component addresses the person as an individual and probes the eternal question of how each of us relates to the cosmos and the universe. The religious component is directed not at the environment but toward each and every person standing as a separate, distinct, and unique individual. It attempts to give meaning to the eixstence of each of us—even if we, individually, do only exist for a brief moment in the great time span of eternity.

So when I speak of Jewish ideas, I am essentially speaking about the principles, beliefs, judgments, feelings, and concepts that have emerged as a result of Jews contemplating the religious component of their identity. I do not include all social, cultural, and political expressions engaged in by Jewish persons. In my judgment, these are not necessarily Jewish ideas, but they can become Jewish ideas to the degree that they incorporate elements of religious thinking.

The most important modifier of Jewish ideas that I have learned as a result of studying history is an awareness of change itself. I think

I always lived with a recognition of change, but I never applied this lesson of change to my interpretation of Judaism and never used it to criticize religious ideas and values. For me, Judaism was always something I accepted as a "bulk package." It was a holy heritage carefully and lovingly preserved by my parents and forefathers; I never felt it was possible to handle it as I handled other parts of my education. One had either to take it or leave it—in each case unaltered. Awareness of change was the factor which turned me toward liberal Judaism; without it, I could find no intrinsic justification for abandoning or modifying inherited teachings, customs, and practices. Without it, it is possible for some Jews still to contemplate the rebuilding of the Temple and the reinstitution of sacrifices. Because if ideas don't change, then nothing once considered holy should ever become obsolete. Even more importantly, without acknowledgment of change, it is impossible to add new ideas or to introduce new forms into our religious life.

The truth is that religious ideas always did change; but change formerly came more slowly and imperceptibly; it could take generations to incorporate a new idea so that, for the average person, the process of change would go unnoticed within a lifetime. There are many ideas in rabbinic Judaism that biblical Judaism simply did not know. The Rabbis could declare, for example, that all Jews must believe in the world to come and its meting out of reward and punishment. Yet it was perfectly possible for biblical Jews to believe otherwise; the Sadducees continuously rejected this notion, and there is no affirmation of it in the Bible; on the contrary, there is denial of any meaningful life after death.

I am not advocating the addition or subtraction of ideas just for the sake of novelty or change. We are talking, rather, about adjustment in our religious understanding in the face of new knowledge, new conditions, and new opportunities.

The ancients had a static view of time; they used history mainly to explain how the present state of affairs came about but had little interest in future developments. For them, the future consisted of maintaining the present conditions as they had them in an unchanging fashion. Thus, for example, the Babylonians wrote myths and epics to explain how their gods came to be and how their forefathers came to settle in their land; but there was no discussion of the future. The building of the Mesopotamian city-states and the worship of the gods therein was felt to be a worthy end product, not requiring further modification or development.

The same perceptions were shared by the early Hebrews as well. The early books of the Pentateuch relate history mainly to explain how the conquest and settlement took place. These were necessary steps for the establishment of the worship of the Lord, and once this was accomplished, there was no reason to think about future developments.

From time to time, there were wars and cataclysms which shattered the static calm of the present. But these disturbances merely interrupted established routine; once they were past, it was only necessary to restore, rebuild, and continue the situation that existed before the unhappy interruption. The ancient Sumerians, for example, considered wars and cataclysmic destructions to be the anger of the gods. Once their wrath was vented, they picked up and rebuilt their cities and worshipped the same gods as before.

The prophets of ancient Israel were the first to look to the future. Much of what they said was uttered in the face of impending doom and destruction, for the prophets anticipated the distintegration of their present order. A great many prophetic speeches deal with restoring the land after this destruction. These sentiments are similar to the Sumerians looking forward to the restoration of their destroyed cities; they look forward to an end of wrath and a return to God's favor. But some of the prophets also turned their vision to a more distant future—realizing that the present is imperfect and that the restoration of the present condition after the destruction would likewise be imperfect. Instead, they looked to the day when all mankind would solve their basic social problems and live in peace and harmony together.

Not only did the ancient world have a static view of history; they also had a static view of knowledge. There was nothing new under the sun; all things that could be known were known already. The process of education consisted of learning from a teacher the stored-up knowledge and lore transmitted by the ancient masters. Their attitude to knowledge and learning was thus backwards looking. What was old was better than what was new; and it was imagined that the former generations were wiser and better than the present-day persons. We see the impact of this view repeatedly in biblical Judaism, where the earlier men have ready access to God, speaking with him without amazement at their being able to do so. Later figures have more limited access to God; direct speech gives way to indirect communication by visions, dreams, and augury. By the end of the biblical period, contact with God has ceased altogether; later holy men like Ezra, Nehemiah, and Mordecai did not possess any form of communication with Heaven.

What we find in the Bible, we also see among the pagans as well. The earlier heroes were able to be in intimate contact with the gods; many of the epical kings in Sumero-Babylonian mythology like Gilgamesh, Adapa, and Etana speak to and freely interact with the gods. But later generations made no claims for direct communication; they could only hope to know the will of their gods through dreams, divination, astrology, omens, and the like.

The Rabbis of the Talmud were impressed with the distance between their own experience and the stories of the biblical figures who seemed to know God so intimately: נתקטנו הדורות they said—the generations have become progressively smaller in spiritual stature. If our forefathers were men, then we are like animals by comparison; if we insist that we are men, then our forefathers must have been angels and not mere mortals like us. This attitude of feeling ourselves small in relation to our forebears is a common one and no doubt has strong psychological links to the universal experience of each of us having once been a very small, helpless child in a world inhabited by large powerful adults. I remember once when I was excavating at our dig at Tell Gezer in Israel. We were digging up what experts told us were large animal bones—perhaps the remains of an ancient feast. One of our Beduin workmen told me, however: "These are not the bones of animals; they are the bones of a human being. Our forefathers were not small like us; they were once very tall." He might have been quoting from Genesis 6:4, "The giants were on the earth in those days and also afterwards; it was when the sons of God came in to the daughters of men and they bore children to them. These were the ancient heroes, the men of renown."

This static view of knowledge has begun to change because of the scientific revolution which started with the Renaissance and which gathered steam with the onset of the Industrial Revolution. We now know that knowledge is not static but that it expands and grows. In the present day, we look forward to learning what our teachers could not have taught us. We recognize the possibility of increasing our data and information. In our thinking, today's facts are only temporary constructions; we are ready to reformulate and restructure our understandings if and when new data will be forthcoming and require it. This is in marked contrast to the ancient way of thinking, where facts are what has been received and transmitted by the great teachers of the past. The changeover in the process of education and knowledge is, I think, one of the main reasons why religious ideas are today under stress. Religious teachings normally take their validity from past authority and seldom appeal to present understanding for validation. Our religious teachings are a living heritage from pre-scientific cultures, and these ancient and classical systems traditionally looked backwards rather than forwards for their ultimate authority to command.

Many modern religionists, caught in the "squeeze" between the old texts and the new expanded knowledge, vainly try to find the new and recent ideas and developments in the Bible texts. They attempt to find the airplane in Jeremiah, electricity in Ezekiel, or détente in Daniel. These are, in my judgment, pathetic efforts to make one time-bound book speak for all ages. There is no reason to expect the Bible to encompass all of time.

But let us not look down on the ancients in a patronizing fashion. Our religious ideas may have first been packaged and presented in a pre-scientific setting; many of the ideas can be criticized, and many are obsolete; but it would be a mistake to think that we have super-seded all of our religious traditions and that we are able to replace them with adequate substitutes. I see a need for humility.

It seems to me that in many ways we do not know more than men did six thousand years ago. We still cannot answer with any greater certainty the basic questions of our existence: Why are we here? What is the purpose of our life? Is there a thinking, reasoning power greater than ourselves? What is our relationship to this greater power if it does exist? We have managed to disprove and disqualify many of the answers that various religious systems have proposed in the past. We know now that the operations of nature do not represent the decisions of independent forces or powers. The moon is not an animate or live deity; the wind and the rains are not controlled by some logical power; and earthquakes do not represent the decisions of an independent god. We have likewise come to recognize that the inner voices and dreams inside of us emanate from our psyche and are not the external communication of God; it is our own hidden, unconscious brain and not the deity who speaks to us inside.

We have disproved old answers, but we still have no new ones to replace them. The old questions remain. We have come to realize that God does not reside in places formerly assigned to him, but we still do not know exactly where the place of His Holiness is.

I believe that the genesis of religious awareness and mankind's first thoughts about God arise from the contemplation of the natural environment. The regular and rhythmic operations of natural law, the predictable and periodic actions of natural forces opened man's eyes to the presence of a larger and more powerful intelligence. It is very much like the archaeologist who comes upon artifacts and buildings which have remained without any trace of the people who once lived there and made the objects. The archaeologist can tell by the conscious designs and the use of geometric shapes and forms that intelligent beings must have fashioned these articles and buildings even though they are absent from his vision. So too, man confronts nature. The regular shapes, the repeated motifs, the predictable patterns and movements, all the natural laws, suggest a plan fashioned by a great designer and builder. The constructions are visible, but the master craftsman is not.

Biblical Judaism placed all of nature under a single monotheistic control but otherwise did not lose that sense of awe that men have always felt when confronting natural forces. When God answers Job out of the whirlwind and tells him, in effect, "Who are you to challenge me?" He punctuates Job's ignorance by reminding him of the powers, movements, and forces of nature that are under his command, whose workings and designs Job can never fathom. "Where were you when I laid the foundation of the earth? Tell me, if you have understanding. Who determined its measurements—surely you know. Or who stretched the line upon it?" (Job 38:4–5). And again: "Can you bind the chains of the Pleiades or loose the cords of Orion . . . Can you lead forth the constellations in their season, or can you guide the Bear with its children? Do you know the ordinances of the heavens? Can you establish their rule on the earth?" (Job 38:31–32). And finally, "Is it by your wisdom that the hawk soars, and spreads his wing toward the south? Is it at your command that eagle mounts up and makes his nest on high?" (Job 39:26–27). The author of the Book of Job confronts Job with his finitude by reminding him of the awesome and unfathomable powers and patterns of nature.

Surprisingly, the Bible does not always make a great use of the imagery of nature when describing the power of God. There are, to be sure, passages like the one in Job and in the Psalms where God is celebrated in terms of his power and control over natural forces. But these are not the major themes. What we find instead is the picturing of God in anthropomorphic terms—king, judge, warrior, and, occasionally, father. The image of God as father becomes increasingly more favored in post-biblical times and is frequently used by the Rabbis. There is a definite favoring of the anthropomorphic social setting and a movement away from the setting of nature. The movement to anthropomorphism is not peculiar to Judaism, and it can be demonstrated in the pagan religions as well. The primitive religions of hunters and food-gatherers are largely centered upon the natural environment and frequently associate animals, plants, and natural phenomena with their gods. The religions of food-producers— the farmers and shepherds—turn increasingly to human images which come out of the more elaborate systems of social and governmental control that these groups develop. The food-producers are concerned with establishing order and plenty out of the impersonal forces of nature. Domestication of plants and animals consists of "bending" or altering nature to the advantage of man's needs. These societies look at God in terms of human needs and thus increasingly come to personify the divine forces in terms of the human agencies which control and manage the affairs of their society, its government, maintenance, and protection.

I think we can see from here that the personification of God is ultimately a matter of metaphor. God himself remains an unknown and unknowable force whose accurate description is beyond the powers of human comprehension and experience. Judaism, like other religions, has therefore attempted to describe God by means of images congenial to its own human understanding and experience. In the Torah, Moses, who of all human beings is said to have approached closest to knowing God, is described as seeing the back of God but not his face—for no man can see his face and live: "And the Lord said: Behold there is a place by me where you shall stand upon the rock; and while my glory passes by, I will put you in a cleft of the rock and I will cover you with my hand until I have passed by. Then I will take away my hand and you will see my back; but my face shall not be seen" (Exod. 33:21–23). This is obviously a metaphoric attempt to convey an unusual degree of intimacy and familiarity with God and cannot be taken literally. The same can be said of the passage that relates that Moses, Aaron, Nadab, Abihu, and the seventy elders saw the God of Israel, "and there was under his feet like a pavement of sapphire, like the very heaven for clearness" (Exod. 24:10). We now know that the cherubs and other fabulous creatures seen by Ezekiel surrounding a glowing king seated on a throne are similar to images also cherished by pagans when they came to venerate and portray their own deities. These winged animal creatures are not incomprehensible as the Rabbis taught; they would have been very well understood by the Babylonian Jews to whom Ezekiel spoke as well as by their pagan Babylonian contemporaries. It would be a mistake for one to take these descriptions in a literal fashion and hope to locate sphinxes, gryphons, and other fabulous monsters in a heavenly throneroom.

If you were to ask me, from my perspective on history, what is the most unique idea of Judaism, I would have to answer: the Jewish emphasis on a moral universe. This concept, asserting that there is cosmic significance to man's social concept of right and wrong, has no parallel in the ancient world. Not that the pagans were immoral. People often say that the Bible gave morality and justice to the world. They are wrong. The pagan cultures had a very lofty concept of justice and taught that right was better than wrong. But the pagans never imagined that the gods were so vitally interested in the affairs of mankind to the degree that a man's unjust act against his brother could upset the world order. They would have placed first priority on man's relationship with the gods; once the gods were recognized and cared for, then a man might turn his energies to his fellow men on earth. But the prophets of ancient Israel proclaimed that there was no use in praying to God or offering him homage if the worshipper had failed to do justice to his fellow man.

I do not think that observation of nature could have inspired this prophetic evaluation of the significance of justice. Nature is impersonal and moves on inexorably. Justice or lack of justice for an individual seems to have no place in the life struggles of animals and plants. The pagan view of great and powerful gods who are only sometimes concerned with man fits better with our experience of nature than does the prophetic notion of a god who prefers justice among men before his own worship and sacrifice. There is no certain way to explain the origin and development of this prophetic concept. We may call it revelation or we may call it the fruits of man's growing awareness and thinking about justice and the social order. In either case, it is an unexplained leap whose antecedents are uncertain.

In my judgment, this concept of a moral universe represents Israel's main advance over paganism. It tipped the balance of the gods and mankind and, for the first time, put concern for man's welfare ahead of all other theological concepts and duties. Without this concept, the distance between paganism and biblical Judaism would not have been so great. True, the Bible also succeeded in reducing all the divine forces to one; it substituted monotheism for polytheism and demythologized the natural environment. But the vision of man's possibilities would not have been so dissimilar. Each system would have counseled man to make the most of his short earthly existence. The Book of Ecclesiastes (9:7–10) tells the Israelites: "Go, eat your bread with enjoyment, and drink your wine with a merry heart, for God has already approved what you do. Let your garments be always white; let not oil be lacking on your head. Enjoy life with the wife whom you love, all the days of your vain life which he has given you under the sun, because that is your portion in life and in your toil at which you toil under the sun. Whatever your hand finds to do, do it with your might; for there is no work or thought or knowledge or wisdom in Sheol, to which you are going." In a similar fashion, the epic of Gilgamesh (Assyrian Rec. Tabl. X, iii, 1–14) urges the ancient pagans: "Gilgamesh, whither runnest thou? The life which thou seekest thou wilt not find; For when the gods created mankind, they alloted death to mankind, but life they retained in their keeping. Thou, O Gilgamesh, let thy belly be full; day and night be thou merry; make every day a day of rejoicing; day and night do thou dance and play. Let thy raiment be clean, thy head be washed, and thyself be bathed in water. Cherish the little one holding thy hand, and let the wife rejoice in thy bosom. This is the lot of mankind." Only the concept of universal justice permits the biblical author to say (Eccles. 12:13): "Fear God and keep his commandments, for this is the whole duty of man. For God will bring every deed into judgment together with every secret thing, whether good or evil."

I do not claim to have exhausted my subject this evening. This is not a plea for more time but an admission of incomplete vision. I am comforted by our post-Renaissance recognition that knowledge can expand and increase. There is still so much to learn and so much to study, and I am hopeful that this can take place. I had hoped this evening to show you the impact of the past upon the present—how ideas, long forgotten and buried, become astonishingly relevant when they are juxtaposed with present-day ideas and notions. The recapitulation of the past helps define the present by giving contrast and comparison. I think we need to remain aware of the past and its treasures so we do not lose the insights and advances gained by our predecessors. Newness does not necessarily represent an advance, even as antiquity does not always speak with authority. We need to keep hold of the entire spectrum of human history. In this way, we will reap in full the benefits of being an ancient people.

Hebrew Prophecy:
The Challenge and the Hope

SHELDON H. BLANK

The word which I would like to leave you with when I am through is one of sober optimism. I shall be moving in the area of religious thought, Jewish thinking in particular, and quite especially the thinking of the Hebrew prophets, whose overall mood I can best characterize as sober optimism.

When I announced as subject "Hebrew Prophecy: The Challenge and the Hope," I had in mind the somewhat contrary natures of sobriety and optimism, both of which natures abide side by side in Hebrew prophecy. I am saying the same thing in other words when I say that the religion of our prophets was a "demanding faith"— yes, the "faith" that purpose guides our world, but recognition, too, that demands are equally present, "demands" upon our ways and deeds.

But the religion of the prophets is no isolated phenomenon. What is said of prophetic religion may be said for religion in general. Religion is both stern and gentle.

Allow me to quote from a Blank book—a question and an answer.

Dr. Sheldon H. Blank is Nelson Glueck Professor of Bible and Editor of the *Hebrew Union College Annual*.

The question: "What does a man's religion *do* for him?" The answer: "It does at least two things—more perhaps but two in particular; when a man is lost in doubt his religion gives him confidence, when he is becalmed it beckons him on to nobler efforts. . . . Religion is a consolation, surely. It is shelter in a storm, stability in a shifting world, a source of strength in weakness, of certainty on slippery ground, of comfort in grief, of hope in sickness and despair. Religion is this, but this is not all; it is something else and different too. It is also law and authority. It deals in imperatives: 'thou shalt' and 'thou shalt not'; it speaks of right and wrong, of duties and responsibility; it is challenge and demand. Religion has at least these two appearances. We might call the one 'comfort,' the other 'conscience.' Religion is the source of both—the source of 'ease' and of 'unease'—and both are represented massively in the writings of the Hebrew prophets." So far the quotation—and my theme.

If I speak of Hebrew prophecy you will know what I mean. You will know, first of all, that I am talking about the Bible, our Bible, the Hebrew Scriptures, also known as the Old Testament. You will know that I am talking with some pride and satisfaction of some people whom we call "prophets," persons who lived centuries ago— before the flowering of Greece, the spread of the Roman Empire, the rise of Christianity—men whose words have become a valued segment of our Jewish heritage. We find the prophetic books, as you will know, in the central section of our Bibles between the "Torah" on the one side and the "Writings" on the other—the *nun* in the acronym *Tanach*. And this is not simply a matter of location in space; it is a symbol as well. To my mind, and in the thinking of most American Reform Jews, the prophets are of central significance. In a real sense the books of the prophets are the heart of our Bible.

You will recognize the names of certain ones among these prophets: Amos and Hosea, Isaiah and Micah, Jeremiah, Ezekiel, and the great prophet of the Exile, whose name we do not know and whom we simply call the Second Isaiah. They are not, of course, merely names of books—these were real persons who moved among our people in Bible times—failures in their day, magnificent failures— giants of the spirit in the perspective of history.

Perhaps we should pause another moment over the words

"prophet" and "prophecy." When we say that the prophets "prophe-sied," we are not thinking of matters like tomorrow's weather or the stock market. Prophets did, of course, predict; they spoke about the future and this was their concern. But it was their insight, not their foresight, that made them great.

Some of you may remember—not many because you are too young —a gala affair here in 1947. It was at the inauguration as President of the Hebrew Union College–Jewish Institute of Religion of my friend, the late revered Nelson Glueck. The principal speaker was Dr. Leo Baeck, and he used a phrase to set off his theme which was worthy of these prophets. "No survival," he said, speaking of the future—yes, the future—of our Reform Jewish movement, "No sur-vival without revival"—a prediction, to be sure, but his concern, like that of the prophets, and ours, was that we, his people, should choose to survive—choose life.

That was the high and holy purpose of the Hebrew prophets. They addressed themselves to the future, not as clairvoyants or fortune-tellers, but with the frantic desire to so move their people that they might have a future. Whether the prophets spoke of future glory or looming catastrophe, they did so in order to achieve survival.

We will be considering the ancient yet ever new message of those prophets, in which were mingled hope and challenge. Their religion, and consequently ours, is both of these apparent contraries, each for itself and in tension with the other, but also blended in dynamic union —a sober optimism, a demanding faith.

Now, the prophets were very forthright, plain-spoken men. That sentence is somewhat mildly and politely phrased. If I were to speak as plainly as they did, I would say that the prophets were fractured ceramics, crackpots, fanatics with a one-track mind. They were seldom lost in indecision by reason of ambivalence. They knew what they stood for and they let it be known—very unpleasant people. You wouldn't want one in your living room. So we may not suppose that they condemned in one breath and consoled in the next. Condemna-tion and consolation each had its turn and context. We deal with two different life situations when we deal with the two aspects of prophecy. What the prophets of hope and consolation have in common with the challenging prophets of the stern demand is that these as well as those addressed themselves to the spiritual needs of their own times. They did not speak in a vacuum. They spoke in a historical context.

First, then, the prophets of hope. What was the life situation to which the prophets of hope and consolation addressed themselves? Start with an analogy. Suppose with me that the survivors of the extermination camps, from which we now are one generation removed—suppose those survivors, contemplating the apocalyptic scene, beat their breasts and said of themselves: "The fault is ours; we are justly repaid for our sins and shortcomings. We abandoned the ways of our fathers, neglected the *mitzvot,* forsook the *torah.* Yes, we have sinned, we have transgressed, we have done perversely: חטאנו עוינו פשענו, we have nothing more to live for, nor deserve to live"—suppose, I say, the survivors of the Holocaust spoke in that fashion, and I am told that some did indeed wrongly take on themselves that guilt, they then would be a recent analogue for the posture of the Judean captives in Babylonia in the time of the prophet Ezekiel. And we can best understand that prophet's message if we imagine it addressed to such a life situation.

How did Ezekiel meet that situation? He was, to be sure, a child of his own time; he did not say, as we might say: "You have no call to take on yourselves this burden of guilt; you are the victims. Not remorse but rage is the fitting mood." The era had not dawned when a prophet could speak in such a fashion. Ezekiel could only speak in terms of a God who generously forgave. There was more to it than that, but, by and large, what Ezekiel showed them was the shining face, the gracious countenance, of a God who offers his people a future and blesses them with peace.

Ezekiel had many more supportive words for a people in despair. In a quite different situation, calling for quite different strategy, as we shall yet see, the earlier prophets had described what amounted to God the father casting off a renegade people. If that was alienation from the father, what is now envisaged is reconciliation with the father. And God, the father, issues the invitation.

Reconciliation would lead to regeneration—regeneration of the spirit and national rebirth. Ezekiel's language is ecstatic. God's promises, pouring from his prophet's mouth, tumble over each other without order and in rich abundance. "I will take you out of the nations and gather you from every land and bring you to your own soil. I will sprinkle clean water over you and you shall be cleansed from all that defiles you. . . . I will give you a new heart and put a new spirit within you; I will take the heart of stone from your body and give you a heart of flesh. I will put my spirit into you and myself enable you to keep my laws and live by them."

Ezekiel first and later the Second Isaiah intone their rhapsody of redemption. No small part of it concerns land and people. It is wrong to suggest that the religion of the biblical prophets was a universalism which negated the peoplehood of Israel and had no concern for land and nation. That is quite wrong. Their religion, taken as a whole, was nationalistic as well as universalistic. And clearly the prophet Ezekiel, and after him the Second Isaiah, confidently announced national rebirth. That is the meaning of Ezekiel's vision of a valley strewn with dry bones. A captive people, despairing of life, would experience new life, return to its land, and rebuild the old waste places. And that is also the meaning of the Second Isaiah's highway through the desert. When, in an earlier age, this people languished in Egyptian bondage, their God compelled the Pharaoh then to let his people go, and he brought them safely through the wilderness to a promised land. In the thought of the Second Isaiah, that already ancient story will repeat itself. The exiled people will see God's work again as now he reduces the power of Babylonia, frees his people once more, and leads them on a desert highroad to their again promised land—a second exodus.

The rapture grows. God will gather them in from the lands where they are scattered, replant them on their land, no more to be uprooted, tame the wild beasts their enemies, give rain in its season to provide abundance, multiply the herds and flocks—no end of peace and plenty—paradise regained.

And when, only a few years later, a body of Judean exiles did return to Eretz Yisrael, not in great numbers but still a community, they thought of independence, and, because they had never known anything different, they thought of a monarchic state. They rebuilt the Temple and Jerusalem, and they had a descendant of the house of David as a candidate for the throne. But Judea was then, and was to remain, a province of the empire of Persia, and it had to abandon the hope for independence and a king. Yes, the religion of the prophets had room for these national aspirations. And their hope and their faith were so strong that they could even weather disappointment. The shattered hope for state and king lived on as a messianic dream.

The word "messianic" holds many meanings. It is an adjective related to the noun "messiah," and "messiah" means "one who is anointed," that is to say, a king or priest—most properly a king. That is where it all started—in the defeated hope for a new King David in a newborn state. The opportunity was lost, but the hope was merely adjourned—adjourned and sublimated. "Messiah" came to mean a more than ordinary king, a divinely gifted man, a king whom God will send with blessing for his people, for all of nature and all men. Even without an anointed king-messiah, the messianic ideal lived on in the hope that God himself would be the king and the world would enjoy his beneficent rule: *Adonai yimloch le'olam va'ed*, "the Lord shall reign forever and ever." This is the *malkut shamayim*, "the kingdom of God on earth," the "messianic age."

"Messianism" means yet more. It includes all that we label "deliverance," "salvation," "redemption." These words and concepts are by no means the exclusive property of Christianity. They are quite as much our own religious goods, a heritage from these prophets—the prophets with the encouraging smile.

One passage is especially significant. It is a reference to the creator God who out of chaos and void, from *tohu va-vohu*, created and fashioned this world. Of him the Second Isaiah meaningfully says: "God did not so form it that it should revert to that primal chaos, he designed it to be inhabited." Friends: in our day, when men have achieved an awesome power, a capacity to destroy all life on earth with a thermonuclear blast, this thought of the exilic prophet Isaiah is mighty reassuring. Listen: "God did not so form this earth that it should revert to primal chaos; he designed it to be inhabited."

"Purpose," "design," and "meaning"—these are here the operative words. We in our day have fallen prey to confusion. Wasting resources, human and natural; overpopulating our planet; waging senseless wars; polluting the air we breathe, the water we drink; our ears assailed with decibels and double talk; we are quite bewildered.

We can only welcome the reassurance in that prophet's words: "not to revert to primal chaos"—"to be inhabited." They are a guide in our perplexity. So, too, the words of another prophet—the expectation of the end of days. The words are a confident hope, an expectation. This is to come to pass in the latter days, he says: "Nation will not lift up sword against nation, neither will they learn war any more; but they will sit every man under his vine and under his fig tree, and none will make them afraid." Such is God's sure purpose. No war or want: a world reborn.

My title is: "Hebrew Prophecy: The Challenge and the Hope." I have turned it around. I have spoken first of the hope. Or have I? Only if we do not dig deep enough. For a prophet of the stature of Second Isaiah, the very hope contains a large measure of challenge. That is the meaning of the bold figure of speech for which he is famous. He personified the people Israel as a servant—"the Servant of God" he called us—a people chosen to serve, entrusted with a mission, called to be a "light to the nations," an agent in the process of redemption, God's witnesses, his partner in the realization of the hope for a world at peace, designed "to be inhabited."

We miss the point if we think of this prophetic hope as a divine promise whose fulfillment we simply await, supine and expectant. We are intimately involved. Reassured with the prophetic recognition of purpose, design, meaning, in our world, we are enheartened; yet we are not relieved of all need for human effort. So indeed, prophetic hope contains a large measure of challenge.

But we have been dealing in particular with the promising, hopeful aspect of the prophetic message; and prophets were by no means unreservedly optimistic. Consolation is, beyond doubt, one important aspect of Hebrew prophecy; but the face of prophecy was not always soft with pity and shining with hope, to soothe and comfort a bewildered people. In other times, amid other circumstances, that face was grim, with set jaws, thin lips, and angry looks. In fact when we casually refer to "our prophets" or "prophetic Judaism," the chances are that mostly we have in mind prophets of this other mold. If we sometimes suggest that Reform Judaism is prophetic Judaism, whether we do so arrogantly or wishfully, we are probably thinking of the message of the pre-Exilic Amos and Micah and the first Isaiah, and of Jeremiah, who was Ezekiel's somewhat older contemporary, thinking of their threats and stern demand. We reduce their message to a phrase and call it a demand for "social justice."

Yes, these earlier prophets represent the other earlier aspect of biblical prophecy. And these prophets also spoke in a context; they addressed themselves to a quite different situation. The Israel to whom they spoke was not yet a captive people in a foreign land, not in despair, not afflicted with a sense of guilt and self-hate, with the thought that God had abandoned them by reason of any offense of theirs, not in any way a miserable remnant of a people—not the survivors of a holocaust. No, they were at home and living high, enjoying security and affluence. They had other problems—but they did not even know it.

You might catch me up when I say that about their enjoying "security" and "affluence." Because, of course, I am guilty of an oversimplification. Properly speaking, I should say: *Some* of the people to whom these prophets addressed their words were filthy rich. Israel was in fact glaringly stratified, sharply divided between the affluent and the impoverished, with cruel inequities.

We can picture it, can't we? The society to whom those prophets spoke was not all that different from our own. We still have hungry people. Televised starvation reaches right into our living rooms. We have no lack of persons displaced and homeless. The lonely aged, the orphaned and the ill, the underemployed and the jobless millions, the victims of war and injustice and bigotry, victims of a white man's court, corrupt officials, rapacious landlords—all of these and their relations are with us in our place and age as they were with an Amos or an Isaiah.

They are with us even though we so often fail to notice. Despite the heightened exposure through the communications media, we seem to be less aware of their existence than, say, our fathers were a single generation ago, or even than we ourselves were some twenty years or more ago. Are we perhaps yielding our personal interest and concern to another instance? Are we letting the vast federal programs take over and replace us? Social security checks, unemployment benefits, food stamps, medicare, congressional investigative committees, foreign aid—all such programs, good in themselves, seem to relieve us of our individual responsibilities, and we seem glad enough to shrug them off. During my years at the College I have noticed the change. "Social justice" was a watchword once. It is heard less often today. "Social service" was a part of one's way of life. "Religious action" was a rallying point. They have been professionalized now and taken over by specialists—which is all to the good, except that the most of us are in danger of losing our humanity, of selling our souls to computers, handing them over with our quarterly checks to the Internal Revenue Service and the Jewish Welfare Fund or United Appeal. If we are not alert we may yet become brothers to those men of ancient Israel and Judah to whom, some twenty-five centuries ago, the Hebrew prophets spoke their words of challenge—men well fed and contented, callous and complacent.

Those prophets of challenge were not callous and contented; they were men of sensitive nature. They were woefully aware of the pain all about them, and of its human source. They saw, on the one hand, the trickery and the treachery, the venality and corruption of men in positions of power; they saw the consequent perversion of justice, the self-righteousness and complacency of the affluent; on the one hand they saw all this, and on the other, they saw the suffering of the victims, the enslavement and degradation of the impoverished, the silent misery of the poor. All this they could see—must see— because of their sensitive nature.

And along with that sensibility those prophets had an openness to an experience which they called the voice of God. This gave an added depth to all that they were made to see. They saw it all in perspective, both the arrogance and the agony; they saw it all as a part of an ailing society, a condemned structure, cracked and bulging, ready to crash in ruin. But also they saw it as sorrow in the eyes of God. Indeed, that looming disaster was not his desire; not for this did God bring his people from Egypt and give them their land. Or, as we might say, not to perish in one blast did the whole vast sweep of evolving life on earth take its slow course.

These prophets of challenge are among the so-called literary prophets; and what they said is indeed among the finest of the world's great literature. Yet writing literature was the furthest thing from their minds. They wrote noble rhetoric, but rhetoric was not their aim.

What *were* they doing then? They were screaming a warning, denouncing, threatening, pleading, seeking with the last measure of their strength to avert the threatened national catastrophe.

We might be inclined to call them pessimists and be done with it—to dismiss them with an epithet. God as they knew him and society as they saw it were simply incompatible. The nation was doomed—fini! Seeing a prophet raise his hand for silence a contemporary was sure to say: "Oh, oh, here comes bad news." Those prophets surely passed as bringers of evil tidings. But were they indeed mere pessimists? No, it was not just bad news that they brought; it was an anguished plea. The divine message they conveyed was an appeal to God's people: "Improve your ways and your doings. *Enable* me to let you dwell on this land which I gave to your fathers. Choose. Choose a new way. Choose life!" Those prophets rejected what in our jargon we call "phychological determination." On the contrary, they were moved with the confidence that human nature has a capacity for change. Even the prophets who came with threats and censure and grim forebodings had their sights set on national survival. All that they required of their people was conduct in compliance with the social conscience—or as they put it, in compliance with God's demands. God being as he is, a people behaving as Israel behaves is doomed. And yet, God being as he is there is hope. If only the people might change its ways and so enable God to forgive—then there might be a future. That, indeed, was God's desire.

Let me illustrate first with a familiar passage, one we often read on the Day of Atonement. It has the form of question and answer. The question: What sort of a fast does God really want? Is the fast-day to be "a day of mortification," "that a man should bow his head like a bulrush and make his bed on sackcolth and ashes?" And God's answer: "No, this is the sacrifice that I desire: that you loose the fetters of injustice, undo the bonds of the yoke, yes break every yoke and set free those that are crushed. It is that you share your food with the starving and bring the homeless poor into your own homes, cover the naked when you meet them and not ignore the needs of your own kin." If this is the nature of your conduct, the passage concludes, "then shall your light break forth as the morning, and your healing shall spring forth speedily, and your righteousness

shall go before you, and the glory of the Lord shall be your rearward."
This prophet was pointing the way to survival—the toilsome, sacrificial way to survival. So the passage concludes with a joyous prospect—conditional to be sure—but joyous.

The passage has a terribly modern ring. I thought I heard this prophet and his fellows speaking when recently I read the words of a group of economists and food experts concerned for the starving millions. They wrote: "Societies do not survive long in moral isolation or human indifference, least of all on a planet made one by physical interdependence and a shared bioshpere."

"Moral isolation," "human indifference," "physical interdependence," "a shared biosphere"—these phrases have a prophetic tone. They are remininscent of words spoken for God by Jeremiah those many centuries ago:

> I spoke to you in your languid ease;
> You said "I will not listen."
> So have you been since your youth;
> You could not hear me,

or by Amos

> Alas for those at ease in Zion,
> Contented on Samaria's hill!

Another example, another meaningful passage in the book of Isaiah. The prophet there complains that his people have tuned him out; they just can't hear him. This in spite of the fact, he says, that he has brought them a very simple message. He has come to them with a formula for peace. Like almost everyone else, I suppose, the prophet Isaiah ranked peace among man's highest goods. He had asked himself: What way to peace? and had found an answer, a formula which he had passed on to his people—but they couldn't hear him. "This is peace," he had said, and he used the Hebrew word *menuchah*, which means rest, repose, security, peace. "This is rest," he said: " 'Grant the weary rest.' This is security." And if I may interpret his words and expand the formula, I think that this is what he meant:

none have rest, he meant to say, none are secure, so long as others lack security. The way to achieve one's own security is to relieve others of their reasons for insecurity. As Martin Luther King once phrased it: "Injustice anywhere is a threat to justice everywhere."

Isaiah phrased his formula for peace only a little while after a fellow Judean, the prophet Amos had questioned popular fantasy. Encouraged by that fantasy his people were quite unbothered. They knew themselves to be chosen of God, God's favorite among the earth siblings, joined to God by an arrangement—one whereby he sustained and sheltered them from all harm. With an all-powerful God committed to protect them whatever they might do, they felt no lack of security. Had he not brought them up from Egypt, made with them a covenant at Sinai, fed them in the wilderness, led them safely to a land of milk and honey, humbled their adversaries with his miraculous aid? They had no care and no concern—not, at any rate, the affluent among them. But with consummate irony Amos addressed a word to the burghers of Beth-el. Quoted (and interpreted), this is God's word spoken by this prophet: "It is with you among all the peoples of the earth, God says, that I have a most special relationship. You like to hear me say that, don't you? All right, I will say it, and then I will tell you how I mean it. I will accept it as a premise and then I will say what it implies. It means that you are in a sensitive spot; you cannot be low-profile. You are more vulnerable, more than all my other children; with your comfortable self-image you are especially culpable."

Put that in more modern terms and it says: privilege implies responsibility. If we are a privileged people—and I say that we are—we have special obligations. Yes, we are a privileged people: we are heirs of the prophetic tradition. We have *been told* what is good and what the Lord requires of us. Our prophetic tradition is an essential feature of our self-image—but not of our self-image alone, of our public image as well—what the peoples of the earth understand a Jew to be—considering his high lineage and his ancient tradition. Neither in America nor in the State of Israel can the Jew evade his proud destiny, avoid his moral responsibilities.

That is the burden of the message of the prophet Amos. And, in a large sense, it is the heavy burden of the collective message of the prophets of challenge.

When, at the annual meetings of the Central Conference of American Rabbis, the graduates of this College, and when, at the biennial conferences of the Union of American Hebrew Congregation, dedicated Reform Jewish laymen take a humane and liberal stand on social issues—as again and again they do—and then go on to shape public opinion along these lines and to influence legislators and governments accordingly, it is the teachings of these prophets which they implement.

Well, then, we have reviewed the two aspects of biblical prophecy, on the one hand the confident hope, on the other the challenge. We have noted and sensed the distinctive flavor of each. In differing times and circumstances, addressing themselves always to the then current human needs, prophets either consoled, supported, encouraged our people with beckoning hopes and promises, or they rebuked, threatened, and goaded them on with a stern summons to moral action.

And the two manifestly dissimilar prophetic models turn out to be not, in fact, contraries. They have, at least, one common denominator. That common factor is human choice—human effort.

The prophets of challenge, with their stern demand, are themselves sustained with the optimistic assurance that human nature can be changed, and that, if men only care enough, they can in fact avoid the menacing descent into disaster. With the human capacity for good they can choose to live—choose life—a human choice involving human effort.

And as for the prophets with the gentler mien and comforting word, in large part they couple with God's gleaming promise a human undertaking. God will indeed choose his people anew and restore and exalt them—but to what end? So that they in turn further God's wider purpose. Here again the human effort. They did not leave it all to God.

The flavors blend; the tones are a harmony: the challenge and the hope combine to create our Jewish world-view and our way of life, a sober optimism, a demanding faith.

The Uniqueness of the American Jewish Experience

ELLIS RIVKIN

This paper addresses the fact of the one-hundredth anniversary of the Hebrew Union College on the eve of the two-hundredth anniversary of our own country. I want to speak of uniqueness, of the uniqueness of the American experience, of the uniqueness of the Jewish experience, and of the intersection and the fusion of the two as we commemorate the Bicentennial of our country and the Centennial of our College.

What is the uniqueness of the American experience? If one rummages through the long history of humankind, and seeks to categorize the various modes which humankind have designed to govern themselves, and the systems which they have fashioned to maintain and to assure their survival, we discover that there are a very limited number of these systems. Indeed, they can be reduced to four.

The first of these systems I shall call pre-capitalist traditional. The second I shall call nation-state capitalist. The third I shall call operational Marxism. The fourth of these systems I shall call the developmental capitalist. Of these four systems, three of them have proved to be cyclical, while only the fourth system—the developmental-capitalist—is unique, is counter-cyclical.

Dr. Ellis Rivkin is Adolph S. Ochs Professor of Jewish History.

The first of these systems, namely the pre-capitalist traditional, is characterized by ruling elites who are motivated primarily by the drive for political, military, and ecclesiastical power. They are not preeminently concerned with economic growth and development. For them the economic sectors are secondary. These monarchical, aristocratic, and ecclesiastical elites treasure wealth, but they themselves are not the wealth creators. They consume wealth; they luxuriate in wealth; they extract wealth created by others; but they themselves have no inner drive to pursue profit for its own sake. Their major compulsions, their overall ambitions, lie elsewhere. They are driven to exercise power as emperors; they enjoy warfare and military splurges; or, as in the case of ecclesiastical elites, they may be very concerned with the spiritual domains of this world and of the world to come. These elites delight in the pomp and pageantry which go hand in hand with these kinds of pursuits.

Such pre-capitalist traditional societies, irrespective of their distinctive differences, go through a seemingly inexorable cycle. They follow a trajectory of an upward trendline of economic growth and development until it peaks out and then turns downward. This peaking-out occurs with such inexorability because traditional governing elites are, as pointed out above, motivated by noneconomic drives. They thus fail to make the kind of investment in technological innovation, particularly in agriculture, that would provide for sustained economic growth. A point therefore is reached where economic growth peaks out, and a trendline sets in which ultimately leads to disintegration and collapse.

This trajectory, although seemingly inexorable, does not trace a straight line, but moves upward with downward loops, and moves downward with upward loops. But however looping the line may be, no pre-capitalist traditional society has ever sustained economic growth as a normative pattern, or escaped the grip of the cyclical trap.

II

The second system, nation-state capitalism, is a system which began to emerge only in the sixteenth and seventeenth centuries. It is an economic system which must be sharply distinguished from all pre-capitalist systems because the leaders in these emergent capitalist societies were entrepreneurs; they were businessmen; they were individuals who were concerned with profits; they were persons driven to accumulate and augment wealth so as to be able to reinvest. They were committed primarily to making their wealth grow; and wherever this economic system gained a strong beachhead and secure salient, it generated changes so radical that they ultimately dissolved and broke up the old traditional societies by spinning off convulsive revolutions and unseating the old traditional ruling elites.

The first of these grand capitalist revolutions occurred in Holland in the sixteenth-century Revolt of the Netherlands. The second of these occurred in England with the Puritan Revolt in the seventeenth century, while the third of these occurred in France with the French Revolution of 1789.

Following each of these revolutions, society was restructured, rearranged, and reorganized in such a way that the old ruling elites, the old ecclesiastical nobility, the old aristocracy, even the old monarchy, were not totally and completely phased out. There was a dominant kind of reorganization of the structure of society so as to commit its ruling elites, whatever their composition might be, to the principles of capitalistic development and the opening up of continuous economic growth which capitalistic development made possible, but there was no total dissolution of the power and governing prerogatives of the monarchical, aristocratic, and ecclesiastical elites.

At the outset it seemed that perhaps this breakout of a new economic system might carry with it the means by which the cyclical grip might be broken, and the cyclical trap sprung. For unlike the previous pre-capitalist traditional systems, whose ruling elites were not committed to economic growth and development, the new governing elites were committed to the augmentation of wealth as a prime concern. The Industrial Revolution, in fact, generated such fantastic wealth that one could extrapolate an upward trendline culminating in the equivalent of the Messianic Age.

And yet that hope, that anticipation, which seemed so well grounded at the turn of the century, and which found poetic expression in Tennyson's dreams of a parliament of man, an end of war, and the new kind of world being foreshadowed by the Victorian Age, was rudely dashed when World War I brought the capitalist nations of

Western Europe into bitter armed conflict and an exhausting, agonizing, and brutalizing war, which not only left millions and millions dead and maimed but plunged postwar Europe into a basic, long-run downward trendline as sharp as any displayed by pre-capitalist and traditional societies. Cyclicity had again won out. If traditional societies, pre-capitalist societies, were condemned to a trajectory, nation-state capitalist societies were seemingly no less condemned.

III

The third system, which emerged at the end of World War I, was operational Marxism as exemplified by the Soviet Union. This was a peculiar and unique kind of system. It certainly was not pre-capitalist. In fact, it was an uprising against pre-capitalism. But it did not follow the model of the grand, classical, capitalist revolutions. The Bolshevik Revolution was proclaimed as a revolution of the proletariat and the peasants; it was led by a very new kind of sophisticated political elite, the Bolsheviks.

The Bolshevik Revolution was unique in this sense: not only did it develop a new kind of leadership, but it seemed to have no cycle at all. By this I mean that it was a kind of system which started out as a failure, and was incapable of rising very much on its own beyond the low point at which it had begun. To the degree that the Soviet Union did make headway, it was only because from time to time it gained access to Western technology to build its factories, and to Western granaries to ward off famine.*

When we reflect on these three systems, each in its own way underwrites a tragic view of human destiny. It seems to confirm the sad vision of the Greeks, especially as portrayed in the myth of Sisyphus. Sisyphus was condemned for all eternity to push with great effort a rock, again and again, to the top of a mountain only to have it plunge, each time, to the very bottom. No matter what and how

---

*For the absolute dependence of Soviet technology on Western imports and models, see Antony C. Sutton's three-volume *Western Technology and Soviet Economic Development* (Stanford, Calif., 1968, 1971, 1973). Cf. also Herbert E. Meyer, "Why the Russians Are Shopping in the U.S.," *Fortune*, February 1973, pp. 66–71, 146–48. Without the succor which the West has provided, and is providing, the system would have careened violently to its doom.

desperate the effort of human beings may be (so the myth would have us believe), the moment of towering success is the most dangerous moment of all. It is precisely at that point that one can anticipate the downward plunge.

IV

There did, however, emerge a highly unique economic system which gives every evidence of breaking through the cyclical trap. It is an economic system which need not go through this inexorable trajectory. This system developed solely and uniquely in the United States. And since this system is not identical with, although it does resemble, the nation-state capitalism of Europe, I call it developmental capitalism.

In what way does developmental capitalism differ from nation-state capitalism? In the first place it differs in the way it began. The American venture from the outset was a capitalistic enterprise. This was the only country which knew no other kind of economic system. What was transplanted to its shores was the new, innovating capitalistic mode which in Europe was developing within older, traditional, pre-capitalist societies—convulsing Europe to its foundations, tearing it apart with revolutions which gave birth to a hybrid form. It was a hybrid because it fused the traditional elites with the newly emergent entrepreneurial elites. It was also a hybrid because it meshed the capitalist system with the territorial, sovereign nation-state system of the pre-capitalist age. Before there was any capitalism in Europe there had been a territory of France, a territory of Germany, a territory of England, a territory of Italy, a territory of Spain. No matter how often these territories changed hands, no matter how many times they may have been added to or subtracted from, they nonetheless were represented as separate, distinct sovereign enclaves. Consequently, when the capitalist revolutions occurred in Europe, not only did this hybrid of an unfinished revolution emerge, but the capitalist revolutions in these countries were contained by the sovereign territory in which the revolution had taken place. As a consequence, instead of a single continental capitalism, there emerged Dutch capitalism, English capitalism, French capitalism, Belgian capitalism, German capitalism, Italian capitalism, etc. The capitalist revolutions had not dissolved the sovereign territorial nation-states; they had only restructured them.

Not so in the United States. The American Revolution was a unique revolution. It was not a revolution against pre-capitalism. Hence it did not conform to the capitalist revolutions in Europe. The American Revolution was a revolution against an already confirmed capitalist nation-state enclave. The colonists did not rise up against the Britain of Elizabeth or James I, but against the Britain as restructured by the Glorious Revolution of 1688.

The American Revolution was indeed unique. It was a revolution against a nation-state committed to imperialism, a state seeking to maintain for itself a monopoly over the innovating and industrializing sectors of capitalistic growth and development by condemning the colonists to the production of cheap primary commodities. Britain also sought to preserve for itself the lion's share of the carrying trade. The American Revolution was thus an uprising not only against an already existing capitalist nation-state, but a capitalistic nation-state which was imperialistic. And since Britain served as the model for the other European capitalist states, we can refer to the European capitalist systems as nation-state imperialist, in contradistinction to the developmental-global capitalism which emerged exclusively in the United States.

What then was the nature of the American Revolution? The essential nature of the American Revolution was the charting of a path for capitalist development which would lead beyond the nation-state to a continental system of autonomous, nonsovereign states. The unique promise of the American Revolution was confirmed by the American Constitution when the Founding Fathers refused to view the nation-state and nation-state sovereignty as the optimal instrument for economic, social, political, or any other kind of development. Indeed, there was a commitment to a Federal Union, consisting of non-coercive state autonomies, enjoying the right of variation and differences of personal and regional life-styles, yet without any concomitant right to exericse violence against nonconforming sovereign territorial enclaves.

By virtue of this major revolutionary decision, capitalism developed in the United States without nation-state barriers. This development proved that the expansion of territory *per se* required no proliferation of coercive sovereignties as the Americans moved from coast to coast. Indeed, when this assumption was challenged by the southern states with their claims to inherent rights to independent national, coercive sovereignty, a bloody Civil War was fought to disallow this option for all time.

The outcome of this decision was momentous. At the end of the nineteenth and at the beginning of the twentieth century, at the very moment when the nation-state systems of Europe were moving into imperialism, the American system broke through to a new stage of economic development, namely, the stage of mass production. The American system was the only system to transform the automotive industry—and the other industires soon to follow—into a mass production industry.

V

No nation in Europe entered this stage of development until the end of World War II. The reason for this is not hard to find. Nation-state enclaves offered only limited domestic markets. But the mass production of the automobile required wide markets, markets sustained by workers whose real wages and standard of living were going up, and by farmers whose income was likewise on the rise. Only such wide and deep markets could support the mass production of high-cost end products such as the automobile.

Such markets did not exist in England. They did not exist in France. Nor did they exist in Germany. In these countries, capital flowed into imperialism and into underdevelopment. By contrast American capital moved into development. The outcome was remarkable. By moving into the stage of mass production as represented by the automobile industry, profits and wages rose in the wake of the heightened productivity which followed on the linkage of worker to more and more efficient machines.

Added to this was another remarkable and unique feature. In all the countries of the world—and Europe is no exception—the farming class is the most traditional, the most reactionary, and the most resistant to change. To this day farming in most of Europe is still, by American standards, extremely backward; it is still a labor-intensive industry. In the United States, by contrast, from the very beginning, agriculture became a technological frontier; and, at this moment, it is the most technologically advanced sector of the American economy. This commitment to technological innovation enabled the American farmer, who would normally have had limited capacity for increasing his yields, to produce such agricultural abundance that he was able to supply food for growing populations both here and abroad.

This breakthrough to a new level of economic development is a unique achievement of American capitalism. This uniqueness subsequently allowed the United States to move to an even higher level when, at the end of World War II, the American economic system began to move steadily from an industrial to a post-industrial society —the first post-industrial society in the history of humankind. This recent breakthrough was made possible by the discovery, utilization, and application of knowledge—not merely technological knowledge, but knowledge of the most abstract general laws of nature itself.

The day on which $E = MC^2$ was translated into the technological processes which yielded the atom bomb, the age of post-industrial development was ushered in. For once the general and abstract laws of nature could be utilized for the creation of technological innovations, innovations began to be ticked off, as in the computer industry, in generations of three to four years. The most amazing kind of achievements occurred, such as the landing of men on the moon. Unbelievable vistas for tapping knowledge to create all the resources which we need were opened up. Indeed, we are at this moment going through that bitter, painful transition from a dying industrial society—polluting, depleting, and exploiting—to a society whose resources are created out of the laws of nature—nonpolluting, nondepleting, and liberating.

VI

So much for the uniqueness of the American experience. Now let us deal with the uniqueness of the Jewish experience. The Jews have had a very remarkable history. It is an unbroken history that goes back 3,500 years or so. It is also a remarkable history because we Jews began as semi-nomads, but find ourselves today literally on the developmental frontier. That in itself would be uniqueness enough. But in addition, the history of the Jews is the experience of a people whose history has always been played out within the matrix of larger civilizations and within larger cultures even during those brief times when Jews enjoyed independence. But, since the Jews did not enjoy independence for most of their history, they lived out their history in societies dispersed throughout the Western world and beyond. They were thus exposed, as a minority people, to the consequences of cyclicism, and to the vulnerability of a minority to suffering precociously as each society entered the downward stage of its trajectory.

Briefly put, in the pre-modern, pre-capitalist cycles, the Jews enjoyed integrative relationships in all host societies as long as the trendline was moving upward. So soon as the trendline went downward, however, the Jews found themselves, even before the rest of the population, deprived of their wealth, pogrommed, humiliated, and in many regions even expelled. That was the experience of the Jews in all pre-capitalist societies.

Jewish experience with nation-state imperialist capitalism went through an equivalent trajectory. Following on the heels of the extension of capitalism into the Netherlands, England, and France, Jews were permitted to resettle; and following on the triumphant march of capitalism in Germany, Jews on the eve of World War I were well on the way to integration. Indeed German Jews looked forward with great anticipation to the day when Germany would be the model for the rest of the world as to how the talents of the Jews could contribute to the prosperity and the creativity of a great nation. The German Jews glowed with pride as their Germany became the pacemaker of Western civilization. And then the collapse: first the Treaty of Versailles and its catastrophic aftermath. Then, after a few years glimmering with hope, the shattering depression, with a third of the German work force unemployed as the economy reeled toward chaos. Reaping the harvest of despair, Hitler was swept into power as he flayed international Jewry for grinding Germany into nothingness. Capitalizing on his triumph, Hitler stripped Jews of their citizenship, imprinted on them the stamp of racial inferiority, reduced them to nonhuman status, and condemned them to extermination.

We thus find that the Jews have indeed had to bear witness to the tragedy breeded by cycles, and they have had to bear this witness in an even more painful way than their fellow victims. Jews were lifted up again and again to the pinnacle of anticipation, and yet at the pinnacle, doom was just over the precipice. It was as though God had chosen the Jews for disaster, and had selected them to confirm the tragic vision of the Greeks, were it not for the confluence of the uniqueness of the Jewish experience with the uniqueness of the American.

VII

In the course of their experience with pre-capitalist societies, Jews found themselves, for the most part, deprived of the right to own land. Landowning was generally a monopoly of the dominant ruling elite. As a consequence, the Jews became an urbanized people in the Diaspora. Since they were a minority and could not exercise military power or effective sovereignty, Jews did not develop military, political, or grand landowning elites. The Jews, in contrast to their host societies, looked to a scholar class for leadership. Hence, learning and knowledge became the highest value cherished by the Jews of the Diaspora: first in pre-capitalist societies, and then in nation-state imperialist societies.

Consequently, when Jews came to the United States, they came to this country as a nonpeasant class, and they came in vast numbers at the end of the nineteenth century, when industrial growth was rampant. They came over to this country as an urbanized class, but not primarily as proletarians. They therefore did not seek out land to farm; and they did not seek out the factories. They avoided becoming proletarians, even though many Jews, in order to earn a living took up employment in the textile industry. Whereas the non-Jew looked on the factory as a liberating step upward, the Jews viewed going into a factory as a move downward. Hence Jews were proletariat-resistant. They did not take pride in being proletarians; they did not want their children to be proletarians. And in seeking a way out of the proletariat, Jews took advantage of the free educational system which was then developing in the United States in a unique kind of way. Since they did not allow their children to go into the work force at an early age, the generation which followed were nonfarming and nonproletarian.

Jews at the time were not aware of the wisdom of their decision. They could not know then that the knowledge sectors of the economy were to become the cutting edge of the American economy, were to usher in the first post-industrial society in history, and were to energize a spiral of development.

This spiral of development is, in fact, the most unique achievement of the American system, for it makes possible an endless, boundless outward-moving frontier, pushed forward every three to four years, as new knowledge generates generation after generation of innovating technological processes.

This frontier renders imperialism obsolete, since the high profits of the innovating sectors of the American economy allow for the transfer, to societies on the lower levels of the spiral, of the technologies which, for the United States, have been displaced by higher technologies. Such transfers allow, in turn, the recipients, the European Common Market and Japan, to release their former high technologies to societies on the level below them, and so on and on until even the most wretched of the earth are drawn onto the upward-moving spiral. Whereas nation-state imperialism hoarded technologies, developmental capitalism diffuses them.

The United States has thus generated a unique economic profile; one in which the farming population forms only about 4 percent of the working population, in which the proletariat is literally withering away, and in which the upward surge is into the service sector, and within this sector, preeminently in the knowledge of industry. This precocious profile is succinctly expressed in the educational index: approximately 40–45 percent of all college-age youth in the United States go to college, whereas no more than 15 percent of all college-age youth go to college in even the most advanced countries of Europe.

Yet when we turn to the Jews of the United States we discover an even more precocious profile than that of the American people as a whole. Jews are hardly to be found at all in farming. They are almost completely out of the blue-collar working class. Instead they are concentrated more and more in the knowledge sectors of the economy. About 19 percent or more of all college professors are Jewish. And when the educational index of American Jews is calculated, a staggering 80–85 percent of Jews of college age go to college. By virtue of earlier experiences of the Jews which depeasantized them, urbanized them, and elevated knowledge to the highest level of value, Jews settling in the United States drifted into those sectors of the American economy which were to become the most innovating and which were to spin off a developmental frontier which offsets the need for cyclical collapse.

VIII

I think now you can discern the uniqueness of the American Jewish experience. The unique experience of the Jews within pre-capitalist systems had prefitted them for the unique thrust of the American capitalist system. It pressed the Jews onto the developmental frontier, a frontier which is enabling humankind to spring the cyclical trap. For the developmental frontier spins off a spiral of development which, in time, will elevate all humankind to a level of humane existence. And the Jews of the United States are on the cutting edge of this possibility. Fulfillment, not tragedy, may indeed be our destiny.

From the aspect of eternity, is it not truly remarkable that on the one-hundredth anniversary of our College and the two-hundredth anniversay of our country, we should be exclaiming "What hath God wrought!" For long, long ago, in the earliest pre-capitalistic experience of the Jews in the ancient Near East, our forefathers of biblical days offered a unique interpretation of their experience. Restored to their land by the Persian emperor, and allowed to live in it only by his sufferance, gifted leaders in Israel promulgated the Pentateuch which proclaimed that God is One, and the universe His creation. This God had brought into existence a world teeming with diversity, and He had capped His creation with a human individual—male and female He created them. And this individual was given the opportunity to enjoy Paradise unearned, but on one condition: that the individual foreswear knowledge. This Adam and Eve refused to do. They were thereupon thrust into history, where, through the refinement of knowledge, the free choice of good over evil, human beings might regain Paradise, a Paradise earned. And lest the teaching of Genesis be lost, God singled out Abraham to father a people to nurture these teachings through cycle after cycle, and trajectory after trajectory. Each failure mocked their faith, and seemed to cry out, "Your God has doomed you to tragedy. You are the living witnesses testifying to the truth of the myth of Sisyphus."

The Jews nonetheless persisted in proclaiming that there would yet come a day when the sword would be beaten into ploughshares, when equity and justice would reign, and when each individual would see God's image in the visage of his neighbor—a hope belying all which experience was teaching.

But a day did come when, on these shores, a unique breakthrough occurred and a spiral of development was spun off. Here human beings began to tap the mind of God, as they successfully translated the laws of nature into liberating technologies. A collaboration between God and humans had been launched. Drawing on the infinite creative power lodging in the laws of nature and nature's God, we shall, in time, create whatever kind of world we should like to have. Paradise lies just beyond the horizon, on the edge of the developmental frontier, if we but freely choose good, and freely reject evil.

The Jews of America are on this frontier because they clung to their faith that God did not doom humankind to primeval chaos; that if Israel were but steadfast, God would be steadfast; that if a way were found through knowledge to attain felicity, God would not thwart us. Pain, suffering, bewilderment did not ever, for the Jew, spell out an irreversible tragedy. And our faith is now about to be vindicated.

At this moment of rededication of our seminary, a seminary which one hundred years ago was founded in the faith that the Jewish people were unique and that the American nation, conceived in liberty and dedicated to the principle that every individual is worthy of equality and justified in seeking happiness, was unique among the nations of the earth, shall we not proclaim along with the watchword of our faith which has preserved us, "Hear O Israel, the Lord our God, the Lord is One," another watchword for the years to come, "Forward to Genesis."

Reform Judaism:
Evolution or Revolution?

JAKOB J. PETUCHOWSKI

We are proudly celebrating the hundredth anniversary of the Hebrew Union College. Reform Judaism itself is about sixty-five years older than the College. We thus have about one hundred and sixty-five years of modern Reform Judaism—which, to some of us, may seem like a very long time, but which, when judged by the length of the history of our people, is almost a fraction of a second. We are, therefore, still engaged in an experiment; and it is as yet really too early to predict the outcome. Perhaps we are not even so much the experimenters as we are the guinea pigs. The outcome of this experiment will, to a very large extent, depend upon what we ourselves are thinking and doing.

Reform Judaism has passed through various phases, which could be summarized in the following way: We began with an esthetic phase, concentrating upon the worship services of the synagogue. We wanted to make the worship service more intelligible, more meaningful, more beautiful, and more musical. That was about the total program of the first Reformers in Europe. They were not conscious of introducing any new element into the structure of traditional Judaism. In

Dr. Jakob J. Petuchowski is Research Professor of Jewish Theology and Liturgy.

fact, although they were attacked by the upholders of the "old-time religion," for whom anything new was automatically bad, blasphemous, and forbidden, as heretics, the Reformers themselves tried to defend their moderate liturgical reforms on the basis of the Talmud, of Rabbinic literature, and of the sixteenth-century code, *Shulhan Arukh*. In other words, they tried to defend themselves on the basis of the authoritative sources which were accepted by their Orthodox opponents. The first phase of Reform Judaism was, therefore, strictly an *esthetic* phase.

The second stage in the development of Reform Judaism can be described as the ideological phase. The Reformers became conscious of the fact that what they were doing was really, to some extent, a departure not only in the language of prayer and in the music of the synagogue, but also a departure from the world of ideas of the generation of Jews immediately preceding them. Our main consideration will be that ideological phase in the development of Reform Judaism. We are not going to deal with the third stage of Reform Judaism's development, which might be called the *organizational* phase.

All human groupings, organized for political, philosophical, or religious purposes, can be broken down into Left, Right, and Center. Thus, in contemporary Judaism, we have Orthodoxy on the right, Conservative Judaism in the center, and Reform Judaism on the left. But the picture is even more complicated, since each group, within its own organizational structure, has its Right, Center, and Left. And so we have right-wing Reform, left-wing Reform, and mainstream Reform; right-wing Orthodoxy, left-wing Orthodoxy, and center Orthodoxy; and the center movement *par excellence,* Conservative Judaism, has its own right wing, left wing, and center.

When Reform Judaism began its ideological phase in Europe, in the fourth decade of the last century, its thinking was dominated by three outstanding personalities. All three of them recognized the need for reform, recognized the necessity of change, and recognized the necessity of adjusting the Judaism of tradition to the totally changed circumstances of Jewish life. After one hundred and sixty-five years of Reform Judaism, it is sometimes very difficult for us to empathize with the mentality of those who lived at the very beginning of this whole process, of those who really experienced in their own circumstances the radical change from ghetto existence to an existence as full members of Western society. But we have to try to understand what happened then.

The right wing of the Reform movement was represented by a man called Zacharias Frankel—who, however, is no longer listed in the Reform Directory because he became the founder of what is now known as Conservative Judaism. But within the definitions of his own time, Zacharias Frankel would be considered a right-wing Reformer. And then there were two other names, and they, in particular, concern us tonight. One of them was Abraham Geiger, and the other was Samuel Holdheim. If, then, we confine ourselves to what, in later generations, continued to be called "Reform Judaism," we would have to say that the Right was represented by Abraham Geiger, and the Left by Samuel Holdheim.

We conjure with those names to this day; and we, in American Reform Judaism, at least pay lip service to the memory of both of those pioneers. As we shall have occasion to see, we are not always very clear in our own minds as to whether we follow the one or the other, or a combination of the two.

Abraham Geiger, who had a distinguished rabbinical career in various German Jewish communities, tried to be a Reformer *within* the total Jewish community. To make that clear, we have to get into some history, because we are dealing with another barrier facing American Jews and their understanding of what happened in Europe a century ago. In America, where we have a complete separation of Church and State, you can collect five, six, seven, eight, or ten other Jews, and establish Congregation Heavenly Rest in Shemini Atzereth, Kentucky; and nobody is going to stop you. If you want to call yourselves a Jewish congregation, even though your service consists of standing on your heads and reading the Quran in a Chinese translation, nobody is going to stop you—because religious association in the United States is a strictly voluntary matter. The State does not interfere.

In Europe, on the other hand, where there were Jewish communities of long standing—some of them were five hundred years old, others nine hundred years and possibly older—the State recognized the local Jewish community as an official body. Until 1876, when a law was passed permitting Jews to leave the local Jewish community without having to convert to Christianity, the German Jew who did not convert was actually compelled by the government to be a member of the local organized Jewish community—whether he liked what the community was doing or not.

The local Jewish communities were not only addicted to the Jewish tradition in general, but they were also particularly addicted to their *minhagim,* their own local religious practice, which would be different from the religious practice of any neighboring Jewish community. When you pick up an Orthodox Jewish prayer book, printed in Germany, you will find an asterisk here and there; and the footnote will tell you: "In Frankfurt, this prayer is not said," or "In Worms, those prayers are recited in a different sequence." Local religious practice was so deeply entrenched in Europe that when, in 1929, the Liberal Jews of Germany finally got around to publishing their own "Union Prayer Book," the *Einheitsgebetbuch,* the ritual appeared in three different editions—one for Frankfurt, one for Breslau, and one for Berlin.

If you were a Liberal or Reform Jew before 1876, and did not like the kind of services conducted in the official community synagogue, you were, of course, free to establish your own synagogue. But you still had to pay membership dues to the official Jewish community of your town. Actually, only two such synagogues, on an overtly Reform basis, were founded: in 1818, in Hamburg; and, in 1845, in Berlin. But the members of those Reform places of worship continued to be members also of the official local Jewish community.

By the same token, and this happened quite frequently, if the local Jewish community "went Reform"—which, in those days, meant that it introduced an organ, a choir, and an abbreviated liturgy—and you were Orthodox and did not like the official Jewish worship service, you could establish your private Orthodox synagogue. But you were still required to remain a member of the official local Jewish community—until the Prussian Landtag, in 1876, passed the law which made it possible for you to belong to a separatist Orthodox (or separatist Reform) congregation, without having to pay membership dues to the old-established local Jewish community.

That is the setting we have to bear in mind before we can understand what Abraham Geiger attempted to do. Geiger did not want to minister to a sectarian Reform group on the periphery, on the fringe of the local Jewish community. His aim was to work for Reform within the total Jewish community, and to bring, as he would have seen it, the whole Jewish community from the sixteenth into the nineteenth century.

In fact, when Geiger was offered a position by the Berlin Reform Congregation—and that happened twice—he declined the invitation. In doing so, he explained that he was only interested in working with the total Jewish community, not with a sectarian group on the periphery. This meant that, by American standards, we would have to describe Abraham Geiger's religious practice and Abraham Geiger's reformed prayer book as being rather on the Conservative side. And yet, Geiger had some rather revolutionary notions.

Until Geiger came on the scene, there was very little sense of history and of development within Judaism. If you study at a *yeshivah,* an Orthodox rabbinical seminary, to this day, you are sitting down at the same table not only with your New York or Chicago teachers in 1975, but also with Rashi of the eleventh century, with Rabbi Akiba and Rabbi Ishmael of the second century, with the Prophets, and with Moses himself. And all of them will ultimately be made to teach the same doctrine, and to give the same legal rulings. That is the art of *pilpul,* a certain method of traditional Talmud study: that you reconcile all conflicting opinions, and come up with the great and perfect harmony which demonstrates that Judaism has always been the same—whether you touch it in 1000 B.C.E., or in the second century of the comomn era, the eleventh century, the sixteenth century, the eighteenth century, or the twentieth century. Judaism has always been the same! True, there may have been minor changes and adjustments. But a truly Orthodox Jew would not admit—and could not admit without ceasing to be Orthodox—that there has ever been any *real* change or development.

Such was the Jewish intellectual climate into which Geiger was born in 1810. Yet Geiger proclaimed a novel idea—novel in his time, but since then taken for granted by us: that Judaism has always been involved in a process of change and development! For example, the period in which the Talmud originated was a different period from the period in which the Bible originated. Not only were the periods different, but the teachings and the laws were also different—although, according to Geiger, there was one element which remained constant, and that was the faith in the One God of Israel and in His ethical demands. Ethical monotheism is the constant element, the red thread which can be traced through all periods of Jewish development. But the concrete ceremonies and practices, and even the formulations of belief in their detailed applications, would vary from period to period.

In fact, Geiger distinguished between four main periods. The first period was the period of "revelation." That is when the Bible came into being. The second period was the period of "tradition." Geiger was very fond of tradition. Some nonthinking Reform Jews tend to deprecate tradition. They think that tradition is bad, that it keeps us chained to the past, and that it prevents development. Geiger pointed out that it was tradition which was *the* factor responsible for progress in Judaism.

Two illustrations might help to clarify what Geiger meant. The Bible says: "An eye for an eye, a tooth for a tooth." But the Rabbis could no longer believe that it was God's will that, if someone knocks out my eye, my attacker's eye should also get knocked out. That does not help me to see any better. The Rabbis, therefore, argue that, when the Torah writes "an eye for an eye," what the Torah really *means* is that monetary compensation, as determined by the court, must be made to the victim. In this way, the Talmud in the period of "traditon," managed to bring biblical law up-to-date.

Another illustration: The Bible says that a rebellious son is to be put to death. Some of us who are parents may, on occasion, sympathize with the biblical legislator. But for the Rabbis of the Talmud, it was inconceivable that God, the loving Father of mankind, wants rebellious children to be put to death. And so they interpreted the law in such a way that it was, to all intents and purposes, utterly impossible to put that law in operation.

Here, then, we have just two illustrations of how, if one takes Geiger's point of view, the period of "tradition," basing itself on the

Bible, went beyond the Bible. This, then, is the second period in the development of Judaism, a period which, according to Geiger, lasted until the sixth century.

The third period, from the sixth century through the eighteenth century, was the period of "rigid legalism." Geiger's name for it already implied a value judgment. This period took over the teachings of the Bible as modified by the talmudic Rabbis. But it was a period of rigidity in which the liberties which the ancient Rabbis had taken in bringing the Law up-to-date were no longer taken. Anything and everything handed down from the past was rigidly codified and adhered to, and thus determined every aspect of Jewish life throughout many centuries.

Geiger, calling that long period "the period of rigid legalism," made a value judgment. Yet Geiger readily admitted that within that particular setting—that is, in those centuries when Jews were living on the fringe of society, when Jews were not citizens of the countries in which they lived, when they were often forced to lead a kind of pariah existence—it was necessary for the survival of the very spirit of Judaism to clothe itself in the garment of rigid legalism. Only thus was the idea of ethical monotheism able to survive the Dark Ages.

But, by the same token, the period in which Abraham Geiger lived was no longer the medieval period. We are now living in modern times, said Geiger; and the same kind of change which was necessary to move from the period of "revelation" to the period of "tradition," and from the period of "tradition" to the period of "rigid legalism," was now necessary in order to enable Jews to enter, as believing Jews, the new period of free existence—the free existence of the Jew as German citizen, as American citizen, and as French citizen. Consequently, the rigid legalism of the dark Middle Ages would now have to give way to a certain flexibility which would make it possible for the Jew, under modern conditions, to maintain his heritage of ethical monotheism, the red thread which runs through Judaism in all of its various phases.

Yet the changes must not be revolutionary changes. All previous changes had been organic changes, evolutionary changes. They never marked a radical break with the immediately preceding past. Geiger could be very radical in theory. He looked forward to a universal religion of all mankind, a religion which would be monotheistic and ethical, and which would have no use for the particularisms and nationalisms of a distant past. But religion does not exist in the abstract. It is practiced by people. The whole people, therefore, must be involved in the developmental process of religion. This being the case, we must respect the traditional attachments—particularly in matters liturgical and ceremonial—of the people with whom we are working. In other words, what Abraham Geiger stood for was a Reform Judaism which would be the product of an organic evolution out of the Jewish past, rather than a radical break with all previous periods of the Jewish past.

Geiger had a friend and occasional literary opponent, Samuel Holdheim. It would be fair to say that, when it came to ultimate questions, Geiger and Holdheim undoubtedly had the same aims and objectives: a universalistic, denationalized, and departicularized form of Judaism. Yet in practice they differed; and they differed also in their theories as to how Reform was to be brought about. While Geiger wanted organic evolution, Holdheim wanted a radical break with the entire post-biblical Jewish past.

Rabbinic Judaism, for Holdheim, was really a terrible mistake and a terrible disaster. Holdheim accepted the position as preacher of the radical Berlin Reform Congregation, a position which, as we have seen, Geiger had turned down. The Berlin Reform Congregation had an all-German service, with just the *Shema,* the Torah reading, and one or two other lines in Hebrew. By the third decade of the twentieth century—admittedly, quite a few years after Holdheim—it had produced a prayer book of just sixty-four pages, which covered the entire year: Friday night, Sunday morning (the Sabbath had long since fallen by the wayside), two days of Rosh Hashanah, Yom Kippur, Pesach, Shavu'oth, Sukkoth, and special services for both Hanukkah and Confirmation. And all of that within sixty-four pages!

Holdheim had a very interesting theological position. This most radical of European Reformers had basically an Orthodox system of beliefs. Indeed, Holdheim began his career as a very Orthodox rabbi in Frankfurt on the River Oder, where he was famed for the rigor of his halakhic decisions as well as for his profound talmudic learning.

(It is probably a law of life that the more Orthodox one begins, the more radical one becomes in his Reform.)

Once Holdheim changed, he truly changed—although he continued to believe that God revealed the Torah to Moses on Mount Sinai. There was no admixture of biblical criticism in Holdheim's view of the Torah—not even of the moderate kind which would be taken for granted in Conservative circles in America today. Holdheim maintained the Orthodox belief in God's revelation of the Torah at Mount Sinai. But, according to Holdheim, the Reformer, that Torah consisted of two very different elements.

One element was the eternally valid religious law—by which Holdheim meant the moral and ethical obligations which follow from a belief in ethical monotheism. But the same Torah also contained the constitution of the ancient Hebrew commonwealth, a theocracy centering around the national shrine, the Jerusalem Temple, and an officiating hereditary priesthood which was bound by innumerable laws of levitical purity and impurity. The whole ceremonial law of the Torah was connected with that priesthood, even as the priesthood was connected with the Temple, and the Temple with the Jewish State.

But, argued Holdheim, God let that Temple be destroyed in the year 70 c.e. God let that State be destroyed in the year 70 c.e. Therefore the whole legislation, the whole constitution, which goes with Temple and State was put out of commission by Almighty God Himself. It was God Himself who abolished that part of the Torah which contained the constitution of the ancient Hebrew commonwealth. All that remains for us is to be found solely in the eternally binding moral and ethical commandments of the Torah.

A few generations before Holdheim we had another great modern Jew, Moses Mendelssohn. Mendelssohn had claimed that it was God's will that the Jews observe all the ritual and ceremonial provisions of the Torah until such a time when God Himself would revoke that legislation as publicly and as spectacularly as He had originally given it.

What Mendelssohn might have meant is that God would send us steamship tickets to the Sinai Peninsula, assemble all the Jews at the foot of Mount Sinai, and, to the accompaniment of thunders, lightnings, and the sound of the *shofar*, proclaim: "The Law which I gave to Moses and the children of Israel is now officially revoked!" Some such image must have been in Mendelssohn's mind. Now Holdheim came along, and took him up on this. Holdheim argued that the events of the year 70 C.E., when God publicly and spectacularly let His Temple go up in flames and His theocratic State be destroyed, that those events represented precisely the kind of official revocation of the ceremonial law which Mendelssohn must have had in mind.

The practical implications of this, from Holdheim's perspective, may be illustrated by Holdheim's treatment of the Sabbath commandment in the Torah. The Torah says: "Six days shalt thou labor and do all thy work. But the seventh day is a Sabbath unto the Lord thy God. On it thou shalt do no manner of work." Holdheim now argues: "To rest one day in seven is a sign of our creaturehood, of our acknowledgment of God, the Creator. This is a purely religious, and not a political commandment. It is, therefore, an eternally valid commandment. But celebrating the Sabbath on Saturday was merely a provision of the ancient Hebrew constitution, which is now no longer in force. We Prussian Jews live under the Prussian constitution, and not under the ancient Hebrew constitution. According to the Prussian constitution, the official day of rest is not on Saturday, but on Sunday. Consequently, we shall keep the eternally binding religious law about resting one day in seven by resting on the day legislated by the Prussian constitution—which happens to be Sunday." Not surprisingly, therefore, Holdheim's congregation celebrated its Sabbath on Sunday.

If one wanted to be critical of Holdheim, one could say—and it has been said—that whatever Holdheim did not like, and whatever he found to be inconvenient, he considered to have been a part of the constitution of the ancient Hebrew commonwealth; and whatever Holdheim did like was to be called the eternally binding religious law of God's revelation.

Holdheim also had his own very pronounced views on the subject of religious symbols. According to him, religious symbols are a language. As long as that language is understood, a religious symbol is valid. When the language of the symbol is no longer understood, the symbol ceases to be meaningful. This may well be a correct perception—although, when it comes to details, one might wish to argue with Samuel Holdheim. For example, Holdheim abolished the blowing of the *shofar* on Rosh Hashanah, because "our generation is no longer attuned to the symbolic sounds of the ram's horn." Our biblical ancestors understood the language of the *shofar;* we do not. Hence the *shofar* was banned from Holdheim's Berlin Reform Congregation.

We might say that there was a certain arbitrariness about Holdheim's selectivity. But then, is there not a certain arbitrariness about anybody's selection from the vast body of available traditions? Not to select is impossible. Even so-called Orthodox Jews today tacitly make their own selections. Still, Holdheim's case may well be considered as extreme.

According to Holdheim, the greatest mistake made by the Rabbis of the Talmud was their failure to realize that God Himself had abolished the Law. The Rabbis acted as though the old laws were still in force. Those parts of the Law that could not be observed after the destruction of the Temple—laws connected with the sacrificial cult and with agriculture in the Land of Israel—could not, according to the Rabbis, be observed *now;* but they would be observed again in the *future.* They were temporarily suspended, but not abolished. The laws which still *could* be observed *had* to be observed. The Rabbis acted as though there had been no real interruption in the whole legalistic structure of theocratic Judaism. Holdheim, the ex-Orthodox Jew, never forgave the Rabbis for acting in that way—particularly because the Rabbis themselves were on the right track. They were on the right track, but refused to follow it through consistently and logically.

The Mishnah, one of the earliest Rabbinic sources, already made a clear-cut distinction between *mitzvoth hateluyoth ba-aretz* and *mitzvoth she-enan teluyoth ba-aretz,* that is, between those parts of the Law which can only be practiced in the Land of Israel, and those parts of the Law which have to be practiced wherever a Jew might find himself. In effect, Holdheim now said: "Look how close those ancient Rabbis were to the truth! If they had only gone one step further, they would have been Holdheimians. They would have made the distinction between the eternally valid moral and religious provisions of the Law, which apply in Berlin, in Cincinnati, in New York, and in Chicago, and those ritual and political parts of the Law which are now abolished, because Palestine is no longer a theocratic Jewish State."

But, of course, the Rabbis made no such distinction; and, therefore, the Rabbis distorted the very meaning of the Bible. The world thus had to wait for Samuel Holdheim, the true Reformer, to make that radical break, to get back to the basic and pure biblical doctrine—or, at any rate, to those aspects of the Bible which are eternally valid and not confined to the theocratic Jewish State.

We find the counterparts of Geiger and Holdheim in the United States of America—counterparts, but not exact parallels. Isaac Mayer Wise was the founder of this institution, the founder of the Union of American Hebrew Congregations, and the founder of the Central Conference of American Rabbis. If you look at the names of the institutions he founded—the Hebrew Union College, the Union of American Hebrew Congregations, and the Central Conference of American Rabbis—you will not find the word "Reform" in any one of them. They were not founded by Wise as denominational "Reform" institutions. In a way somewhat similar to Geiger's, but perhaps with a great deal less of intellectual sophistication, Isaac Mayer Wise wanted to work for and within the totality of the American Jewish community. His was not going to be a sectarian movement on the periphery of Jewry. He was indeed convinced of the truth of Reform Judaism. He was an ardent Reform Jew; but he also had so much faith in his Reform Judaism that he felt that, once he had succeeded in uniting all of American Jewry, Reform Judaism would of necessity become the ultimate religious philosophy of American Jewry—the only form of Judaism which was feasible on the American scene, in this totally unprecedented New World. First, however, the American Jewish community would have to be united.

In order to achieve that unity, Isaac Mayer Wise, at various points of his life, was quite ready to make compromises with the traditionalist predilections of other American Jewish leaders. At the famous Cleveland Conference, he hoped to obtain the cooperation of the Orthodox by signing a statement to the effect that the Talmud is the authoritative interpretation of the Bible.

Some of the other Reform rabbis who were already in this country never forgave Wise this compromise. They considered it to have been treason to the cause of Reform. While Wise put *kelal yisrael,* the totality of the Jewish community, above his striving for Reform, those others put the striving for Reform above their consideration for *kelal yisrael.*

Perhaps the most famous name in that second group was that of David Einhorn, who played Holdheim to Wise's Geiger. David Einhorn had no use for Reform Judaism as a mass movement which must compromise, and which must make concessions to tradition. Reform Judaism, for Einhorn, was the religion of a cultural and intellectual élite—and not of just any cultural and intellectual élite, but of the *German-speaking* cultural and intellectual élite. Einhorn belonged to that group of people who pooh-poohed Isaac M. Wise's dream of creating a rabbinical seminary in America. How can you train Reform rabbis in America—and in English, yet—when everybody knows that the language of Reform Judaism is German, and its philosophical moorings are German?! And so it was indeed—on the eastern seaboard. (It is amusing how geographies and ideologies change. Today, the Midwest is "Classical Reform," and the eastern seaboard is flirting with tradition. A hundred years ago, the eastern seaboard was "Radical Reform," while the Midwest—and, foremost within the Midwest, Cincinnati—was the seat of the conservative position in Reform Judaism, led by Isaac M. Wise.) The Reform rabbis of the eastern seaboard argued that, if you wanted to have Reform rabbis in America, you would have to send the students to Germany to be trained.

Einhorn himself, though he spent almost a quarter of a century on American soil, never preached an English sermon. The prayer book which he edited in Baltimore appeared in Hebrew and in German. Einhorn also predicted that Reform Judaism would die the moment Reform Jews were to cease speaking German and being steeped in German literature and culture. And he was quite right. The kind of Reform Judaism which Einhorn championed did not, to put it mildly, fare too well once English had taken the place of German as the language of American Reform Judaism.

Yet to think of Einhorn, who in many ways echoed the teachings of his friend Holdheim, as being merely an American copy of Holdheim, the extremist in Germany, would not do Einhorn full justice. Holdheim officiated at mixed marriages, and was proud of it. He even published the sermons he preached on those occasions. Einhorn, on the other hand, the radical American Reform rabbi, was perhaps the most vociferous opponent of mixed marriage ever to have arisen in American Reform Judaism. Einhorn firmly believed that the Jews had a mission to all mankind, that the Jews were God's "priest people" on earth. But if the Jews, through mixed marriages and assimilation, were to disappear as an identifiable group, then the Mission of Israel could not be fulfilled, and God's plan would be thwarted. Therefore, for the sake of all mankind, the Jews must maintain their group identity and their group integrity.

Isaac M. Wise, leader of moderate Reform, and David Einhorn, the radical. How was the conflict between them resolved? Einhorn and his party were victorious. The prayer book which we have been using until very recently, the *Union Prayer Book,* was basically the prayer book which Einhorn wrote. The Pittsburgh Platform, which, for many years, reflected the official position of American Reform Judaism, echoed the teachings of Einhorn (and of Holdheim, for that matter) much more faithfully than it reflected the aspirations of Isaac M. Wise. The man who, after a brief interlude, succeeded Isaac M. Wise in the presidency of the Hebrew Union College was Kaufmann Kohler. Kohler was not only Einhorn's son-in-law, but also his most enthusiastic disciple. Reform Judaism in America, for quite a long time, was content to be the religion of an intellectual and financial élite, which had broken with the old ways and the meaningless traditions, and which recognized only moral, but not ritual, demands as the Word of God. To a very large extent—though hardly quite as largely as its opponents claimed—it had cut itself off from *kelal yisrael* and from too intimate a contact with the rest of the Jewish people.

Today, we are again living in a different world. Neither Geiger nor Holdheim, neither Wise nor Einhorn could dream of either the Holocaust or the State of Israel. Yet those two events have had an immeasurable impact upon the thinking of all of us. They have called into question some of the most basic and fundamental assumptions which had been made a hundred years ago. As a result, American Reform Judaism has forsaken the élitist approach of the Holdheim-Einhorn school of thought, and has rediscovered the *kelal yisrael* orientation of Geiger and of Isaac M. Wise.

All of this, however, does not mean that today's American Reform Judaism has a uniform or monolithic philosophy—let alone a unified religious practice. We are still arguing about the direction in which Reform Judaism is to move. We are again breaking up into Left, Right, and Center.

At issue is the basic question whether Reform Judaism is predicated on organic growth and development, that is, evolution, or whether it stands for revolution and a radical break with the Jewish past. Particular terms of reference may have changed. The specific questions are different now. But at the root of the present debate, and of the present unrest in the Reform Jewish camp, there is the old debate between Geiger and Holdheim, the old dialectics between Isaac M. Wise and David Einhorn.

Reform Judaism—evolution or revolution? The debate continues. The experiment is still in progress. I hope that we shall be granted another one hundred years to pursue this question further.

The theme of this paper is further developed, and full documentation is supplied in Jakob J. Petuchowski, "Abraham Geiger and Samuel Holdheim—Their Differences in Germany and Repercussions in America," Year Book of the Leo Baeck Institute, *XXII (1977).*

Jews in America–
Jews in Israel:

How Shall We Understand
Our Relationship?

MICHAEL A. MEYER

About eighty years ago the well-known Viennese playwright and journalist, Theodor Herzl, deeply shocked by the virulent anti-Semitism that he had observed in Paris at the Dreyfus trial, composed a political tract which he called *The Jewish State*. In that famous manifesto of the modern Zionist Movement, Herzl included the following words:

We have honestly endeavored everywhere to merge ourselves in the social life of surrounding communities and to preserve the faith of our fathers. We are not permitted to do so. In vain are we loyal patriots, our loyalty in some places running to extremes; in vain do we make the same sacrifices of life and property as our fellow citizens; in vain do we strive to increase the fame of our native land in science and art, or her wealth by trade and commerce. In countries where we have lived for centuries we are still cried down as strangers. . . . For old prejudices against us still lie deep in the hearts of the people. . . . Jews are even now constantly shifting from place to place, a strong current actually carrying us westward over

Dr. Michael A. Meyer is Professor of Jewish History.

the sea to *the United States, where our presence is also not desired.* And where will our presence be desired so long as we are a homeless nation?[1]

A year later political Zionism was launched at Basel with the first Zionist Congress, and the thoughts which Herzl had here expressed became the basis of an international movement. But not all Jews, indeed very few Jews in the West, sympathized with what Herzl wrote. Most of American Jewry, feeling very much at home on these shores, was simply outraged.

Two years after that pamphlet, about a year after the first Zionist Congress, in the Hall of the House of Delegates at the State Capitol in Richmond, Virginia, the Union of American Hebrew Congregations held its sixteenth national council. The delegates there assembled, representing nearly one hundred congregations, felt that they had to speak out on Herzl's project. They had no choice but to say something about this new movement that had just been launched in Europe. And so they appointed a committee to draft a resolution on Zionism.

The committee consisted of three members, two of them graduates of the first rabbinic class of the Hebrew Union College in 1883. One was the rabbi of Temple Bene Israel of Cincinnati, shortly to be known as Rockdale Temple, David Philipson; the other College graduate was Joseph Krauskopf of Philadelphia; the third member was a layman, Simon Wolf.

This committee came up with a statement which was then adopted unanimously by all of the delegates. It read, in part, as follows:

We are unalterably opposed to political Zionism. The Jews are not a nation, but a religious community. Zion was a precious possession of the past, the early home of our faith, where our prophets uttered their world-subduing thoughts, and our psalmists sang their world-enchanting hymns. As such it is a holy memory, but it is not the hope of the future. America is our Zion. Here, in the home of religious liberty, we have aided in founding this new Zion, the fruition of the beginning laid in the old. The mission of Judaism is spiritual, not political. Its aim is not to establish a state, but to spread the truths of religion and humanity throughout the world.[2]

Since then some three generations have passed. We have gained historical perspective on what was written by Herzl on the one hand and by David Philipson on the other. It is now possible to say with some confidence that both Herzl and the UAHC delegates have been proven wrong by history.

In what way has Herzl been proven wrong? The founder of political Zionism believed that, with the establishment of the Jewish State, those Jews who would migrate to its shores would enjoy lives of security and tranquility, freed from anti-Semitic oppression. They would be untroubled by anxiety for their present safety and their future well-being. Yet, sadly, the State of Israel, which came into existence in 1948, has not brought that sought-for tranquility and confident hope for the future.

Nor has America turned out the way Herzl expected. Today it seems that the Jews' presence in America is considerably more desired than it was in the 1890s, when massive waves of immigration from Eastern Europe swept onto these shores. Not that anti-Semitism is dead in America today, but it exists less virulently and extensively than it did two generations ago. The result is something which Herzl would certainly not have anticipated: more Jews, since the establishment of the State, have come from Israel to the United States than have made *aliya* from the United States to Israel. Indeed, most recent figures show that even among those Jews who now, if they are able, leave the Soviet Union ostensibly to join their relatives in the State of Israel, as many as one-third, once they reach Vienna, choose to make their way not to Jerusalem and Tel Aviv but to New York and other American cities. Upon reflection, it seems that the danger to Jewish survival in America today comes less from anti-Semitism, as Herzl anticipated, and more from mixed marriage and apathetic indifference.

But if Herzl was wrong in very important respects, so, too, was David Philipson. Few Jews today would say with those UAHC delegates of eighty years ago that America is our Zion. Jews in this country have become considerably more sober about applying such messianic terminology after the tragedy of Vietnam and the revelations of Watergate. America is far too imperfect to be called Zion in the ultimate sense of the word—which refers to a messianic ideal. And in its immediate physical and geographical sense, the word, of course, refers to an actual mountain called Zion in the environs of Jerusalem —a place many American Jews have themselves likely visited as tourists. When one has stood atop a mountain historically called Zion, it becomes difficult to call any other place by that name.

Also, I believe few Jews in America today would say that we are nothing more than a religious community, as did the UAHC delegates in 1898. Ethnicism in America has ceased to be taboo. We no longer have to tell our Gentile friends: "Look, Judaism is just like Protestantism and Catholicism. It is merely a denomination. We differ from you only with regard to certain beliefs and ritual practices." Today we are far more willing to say that Jewish identity is much more encompassing, that it includes cultural elements, the elements of peoplehood, and not simply those of religion. Indeed, much of contemporary life in America seems not to be centered at all upon the synagogue, but rather on some expression of our relationship to the State of Israel. Many Jews who seldom attend religious services express their belonging to the Jewish people by raising funds for the United Jewish Appeal; they participate in the Jewish community through those of its organizations that deal with the needs of the State of Israel.

Finally, the UAHC statement said that the Palestinian Zion was not the hope of the future. And yet, apart from the relationship with this physical Zion symbolizing the State of Israel, I think many American Jews today would find little hope for any meaningful Jewish future at all in the Diaspora. It is our sense of shared destiny with Israel that gives American Jewish life very much of its significance.

If we examine the connection that has in fact developed between American and Israeli Jewry, we may term it a relationship of fundamental interdependence. We need and depend on one another. Israeli Jews must rely on American Jews in a number of ways. Obviously they must depend on them for funds to support social welfare, lest the Israeli economy, already pressed to the limit, crack under the burden of supporting an essential military establishment and also attempting to meet social needs. Unless funds are furnished from the outside, moreover, the unfortunate gap that continues to exist between the relatively better off Ashkenazi minority and the much larger and less well off Sephardi Afro-Asian majority will expand, perhaps leading ultimately to a serious and unbridgeable rift in Israeli society.

Israel also looks to American Jewry as the one sure source of moral support when it confronts a world intent on isolating it and making it into a pariah. When the United Nations can declare absurdly that Zionism is a form of racism and consider it a philosophy comparable in reprehensibility to South African apartheid, Israeli morale requires renewed Zionist affirmation by Diaspora Jewry.

This is likewise a time when Israel is becoming increasingly dependent on American Jewry for its political influence with the United States government, since America has become the only major power ready to support Israel at all. The total weight of Israel's dependence on American Jewry is thus so great that one can say without exaggeration: but for the efforts of American Jewry it is doubtful whether Israel could physically survive—or, if survive, fulfill even a portion of its promise.

Yet at the same time American Jewry is very heavily dependent upon Jews in Israel. It is dependent, first of all, for an added measure of cultural vitality and Hebraic creativity which, however much we try to deepen (as we should) Jewish education in this country, we shall never be able to equal. The Hebraic culture which Israel offers provides us with an important means to resist the assimilation that is born of vacuity.

Israel also presents us with a model of moral resolve. It affords concrete proof of an indomitable will to Jewish survival in spite of the Nazi tragedy. The fact that a Jewish State could arise out of the ashes of the Holocaust—and that it continues to exist despite tremendous odds—keeps a Jewish community from despairing on account of the murder of six million and enables it to continue burning the candles of messianic hope. Thus, even as Israel's future depends on American Jewry, so too does American Jewry require Israel. Without the State it is doubtful whether American Jewry could overcome the pressure to disappear, doubtful whether after the Holocaust it could decide firmly for Jewish survival.

If, then, our relationship is one of such clear and vital interdependence, it is imperative that both sides examine that relationship closely.

Such an examination, I think, must embrace two elements. First, it must include an understanding of our differences, of how American Jews differ from Israeli Jews; and, second, it must include a recognition of our mutual obligations.

To begin with the differences: American Jewry's social composition is not the same as that of Israeli Jewry. Most of us are to be located somewhere in the middle class. We are concentrated in certain occupations, especially in the service industries and in the professions. We send almost all of our young people to colleges and universities. American Jewry thus represents a particular socioeconomic and educational grouping within the total population of the United States.

By contrast the Jews in Israel fill the spectrum of an entire society: the lower, middle, and upper class. All of the usual occupations are represented, and Israelis attain various levels of education. In other words, American Jewry represents a slice of society; Israeli Jewry represents the totality. If, then, it is true that people tend to relate more easily to others who possess the same intellectual, social, and economic background, one must allow for American Jews having far more in common with a particular segment of Israeli Jewry than with Israeli Jewry as a whole.

Moving from the sociological to the historical, I believe that Israeli Jews and American Jews have profoundly different understandings of the Holocaust. For American Jews, the Holocaust does not signify the ultimate futility of living as a minority among non-Jews. If it did, then we would cease trying to exist as Jews in America, where we constitute less than three percent of the population. And yet we do continue living Diaspora Jewish lives, and some of us even believe there is a special purpose in it: that as survivors of the Holocaust, who persist in being a minority within a majority, we testify to our rejection of the Nazi ideology, which wanted to make all the nations *judenrein*. Despite Hitler we continue to exist in many countries of the world, contributing of ourselves to those societies which welcome us. As survivors, we have accepted the task of striving to prevent similar holocausts from occurring in the future.

For Israelis the Holocaust has a different meaning. For them it represents a final proof of Herzl's argument that anti-Semitism can never be rooted out and that even where it seems to be disappearing (as it seemed to be in Weimar Germany), it will recur yet more virulently. That Germany, the technologically most advanced country in Europe, could have spawned the most dreadful manifestation of anti-Semitism is for many Israelis irrefutable evidence that Diaspora existence—in whatever place—faces the likelihood of a similar horrendous turnabout.

American Jews and Israeli Jews also draw upon different periods of the Jewish past in seeking their own self-understanding. For American Jews certain epochs of Diaspora Jewish history supply models for contemporary Jewish life. We look to the great talmudic academies of Babylonia, the Golden Age of Hebraic creativity in Spain, and in this Bicentennial year especially to American Jewish history.

But for Israeli Jews Diaspora history cannot serve as an identity model the way it does for us. Israelis turn to other periods of the Jewish past with which they can feel a closer affinity: those times when the people dwelt in its own land. Israeli schoolchildren study carefully the ancient monarchy, when King David, King Solomon, and their successors ruled; they learn about the period of the Second Temple, especially those years when, under Hasmonean rulers, the nation enjoyed political independence. There follows a long gap until modern Zionism and its return of the people to its land. Since we draw upon different periods of the past, we establish different historical identities.

There is also that dissimilarity which necessarily exists between a minority and a majority. Unless it is ghettoized, a minority cannot help but be influenced by its environment. The manner in which it is able to exist depends less on itself than the attitude of the majority. As a result, modern Diaspora Jews have always been very self-conscious, very concerned about what the Christians think. We have a tendency to see ourselves as we believe the majority sees us; we are not the shapers of our own self-image.

As American Jews we are profoundly influenced by what occurs in a society of which we are a part but over which we have little control. Trends in Christianity invariably influence trends in Judaism. At a time when more people affiliate with the churches, larger numbers of Jews join a synagogue; when Christian theology becomes existentialist, Jewish theologians seek an equivalent understanding of Jewish faith. If secularism should one day become wholly dominant in this country, it will be very difficult for any kind of religious Judaism to survive. Should ethnicism decline sharply as a value in American society, Jews will be hard pressed to maintain their identity as a separate people.

A Jewish majority, as we have in the State of Israel, is in a very different position. It enjoys a certain amount of freedom from concern about the effects of its actions, at least insofar as they do not extend beyond its borders. To be sure, foreign influences are present in the life of any nation, and certainly in that of Israel, but the fact remains that, as a majority, the Jewish community in Israel is far more able to shape its own character.

It seems also that there are certain sensitivities which are the product of life as a minority in Diaspora. Most Israelis today are native-born, including for the first time a Prime Minister of the State of Israel, Mr. Rabin. It has been my experience as a Diaspora Jew spending an extended period of time in Israel that communication was generally easier and more profound with those Israelis who had themselves been born in the Diaspora or, if they were native-born, had spent a good deal of time outside of Israel. I found it much more difficult to converse meaningfully with Israelis who had never had the experience of being a minority.

We American Jews sometimes like to say, with Mordecai Kaplan, that we live in two civilizations, one Jewish, the other American. Yet in fact most of us live almost entirely within American civilization. We use the English language; we are subject to all the cultural influences of our society. For all but a very few, the sources of our tradition in the Hebrew language remain unfamiliar. Our Hebrew is limited to knowing a few prayers and perhaps a stray word or two of modern Hebrew.

But Israelis live in a Hebraic civilization; and however much that civilization is open to cultural influences beyond the borders of Israel, however far it is from being pure, it nonetheless possesses a certain linguistic connection with the traditional Jewish sources. Of course Israelis, particularly the educated ones, know English, but there remains nonetheless something in their way of thinking which is Hebraic and which separates them from the speakers of English who have grown up in an English cultural environment. I think we would err if we underestimated the significance of this linguistic barrier.

Nor is it possible to ignore that, from year to year, the specifically Israeli experience—Israeli history—grows ever longer while the common experience that nearly all Jews shared in the Diaspora before the State recedes into the background. Israelis live in a historical environment that Diaspora Jews share in only vicariously. In the course of time, as more and more Israelis become native-born and have less direct acquaintance with the Diaspora, the shared experiences of the pre-State period will recede ever more and the possibility loom of Israelis and American Jews growing culturally ever further apart.

We also understand religion very differently. For American Jews religion is voluntaristic. We join a synagogue or we remain unaffiliated. We tend to think of religion not simply in terms of traditional belief and practice. For us it involves a variety of theologies competing with one another, an important element of social justice flowing from prophetic imperatives, and a messianic vision that embraces all mankind.

For most Israelis religion is far more narrowly conceived. With the exception of the members of the small Reform and Conservative congregations and a few others, it is understood as Orthodoxy. They see it represented as part of the power structure, as an alignment of political parties which seek to gain tangible rewards for their members and endeavor as much as possible to impose the traditional laws of Judaism upon the populace at large. Most Israelis—whether Orthodox or secular—perceive religion as a matter of observance, not response to moral demands. Whether you are considered *dati* (religious) or not depends less on your commitment to certain moral imperatives than it does on the degree of ritual observance.

It seems also that the religious parties of Israel have very greatly neglected the universalistic elements in the Jewish religious tradition and have stressed an exaggerated particularism instead. To a large extent it has been the religious leadership that has argued most vehemently for unlimited settlement on the West Bank, for a refusal to give up any territory since, so it is believed, the entire land is holy soil. It is those who represent religion that seem most easily to have forgotten that moral claims are not limited to Jews alone.

To put it in the broadest terms, we are simply different kinds of Jews. We have to recognize that fact and the patent folly of one side or the other trying to make its partner over in its own image. Even as we favor religious and ethnic pluralism in the United States, we have to recognize and affirm a similar kind of Jewish pluralism, a pluralism of identities falling into two major types: the Israeli Jew and the Diaspora Jew—with a host of variations within these two principal categories.

Having said this much about our differenes, I do not therefore intend to imply that the relationship must necessarily be weak. Quite the contrary. It is only after we have honestly examined both our mutual dependence and our dissimilarities that we can speak of building a genuine, close relationship.

The foundation of such a relationship consists of obligations which we owe to each other. Let us begin with the question: What can American Jews legitimately ask of Israel? First and most basically, I believe that American Jews can ask of Israeli Jews that they respect our deep commitment to the survival of the Jewish people even though we have chosen not to dwell in the State of Israel. We can ask of Israelis that they not assume an American Jew who does not intend to make *aliyah* is on that account any less concerned with the physical and spiritual future of the Jewish people. If he does make *aliyah,* well and good; Israel certainly needs such skilled and educated individuals as American Jewry can offer. But if the American Jew chooses to make his Jewish life here, Israelis must not deprecate his decision. We can ask of Israeli Jews that they recognize American Jews as equal partners in a larger entity called *am yisrael,* the people of Israel, in which they and we both have a role to play.

American Jews can further ask of Israeli Jews that they allow us to make our voice heard with regard to those issues of Jewish life that, though they pertain principally to the State of Israel, ultimately affect all Jews wherever they be. This includes certain basic decisions of Israeli foreign policy, especially those that bear directly upon the nature of the Jewish State. I believe that American Jews have the right to discuss the fundamental issues here as Israelis discuss them freely in Israel. American Jews should be sufficiently concerned with these questions to consider the options offered by a variety of Israeli politicians. They need not assume that what the government in power holds on a particular issue is necessarily good in the long run for the physical and moral survival of the Israeli state or of the Jewish people. American Jews should feel free to support those forces in Israel which they believe are aiming most closely at the kind of solution to the Israeli-Arab confrontation which will both assure Israel's security and be in the ultimate interest of both sides.

Likewise with regard to certain domestic matters in the State of Israel, those which affect us directly, we should have the right to make our voice heard—not to determine issues, but to throw the weight of our opinion into the scale of decision. One such matter is the question of religion in the State of Israel. When liberal Judaism is not allowed equal status, when decisions regarding who may marry whom are made in a way which from our liberal perspective is wholly wrong, when religion is almost totally divorced from public morality, then as Reform Jews we have an obligation to support those forces within Israeli society—especially the fledgling liberal movement—which are attempting to bring about a very different conception of religious Judaism in the State of Israel.

But there is another side to the equation, and that is what Israeli Jews can justifiably ask of us. In the first place, they can with full justification demand that whenever American Jews support a particular Israeli foreign policy—with regard to the Palestinians, for example—that they fully appreciate one enormous point of difference: Israeli Jews put their lives on the line, American Jews do not. There must, therefore, always be a certain reluctance about our speaking out, an awareness that though we want our voice to be heard, it must sound faint before the opinions of those who daily face the prospect of offering their own lives or witnessing the death of their kin and companions.

Quite obviously, Israeli Jews can and do ask of American Jews the financial support which Israelis need to make a difficult life bearable, to resist despair, in spite of a declining standard of living. Israel has the right to insist that American Jewry's wealth imposes severe financial obligations. If American Jews really take Israeli survival seriously, then they must meet those commitments.

In addition, although Diaspora communities should in general feel free to reject dictates from the State of Israel, an exception is created during moments of crisis, when another Holocaust may seem a real possibility. Examples are the eve of the Six Day War and the entire Yom Kippur War. At such times American Jewry must respond quickly and massively; there is then no time for discussion. At the point of peril, Israelis can justifiably demand of American Jews an immediate expression of their absolute commitment to the survival of the State of Israel.

Finally, Israelis can ask that American Jews exercise maximum influence on American public opinion, on Congress, and on the President in those areas which are vital to the State of Israel. Such influence, however limited, is absolutely essential at a time when Israel has no major ally apart from the United States, a situation unlike the 1950s, when it could rely on France and Great Britain.

Israel can ask of American Jewry specifically that it champion United States military aid to Israel—not soldiers, but the weapons Israel requires to defend itself. We are also required to persuade our government that it undertake diplomatic offensives to restore the badly eroded position of Israel in the world community of nations. Without the support of the powerful United States, Israel cannot hope to win back nations heavily dependent on the producers of Middle Eastern oil.

It is, of course, possible that in attempting to meet these obligations, especially through the exercise of political influence, American Jews will raise the level of anti-Semitism. Yet I am persuaded that that possibility must not deter us. I believe American Jewry is by now sufficiently secure that it can afford to take certain risks, and it must take them when the alternative endangers the physical survival of the State of Israel.

Let me conclude with a more elevated notion. Ideally, I believe, Diaspora and Israeli Jews should complement one another in a spiritual sense. The Israeli, living on the ancestral soil, reminds us Diaspora Jews of our Jewish particularity. His reestablishment of a Jewish State after two thousand years represents a great realization of Jewish hopes, a fulfillment of ancient promise; a few even say the beginning of messianic redemption. The new Jewish commonwealth, which the Israelis have created and in which they live, is for us American Jews tangible evidence that the connection between God, the Torah, the people of Israel, and the land of Israel has not been broken.

On the American Jew, living in a country dedicated two hundred years ago to Enlightenment principles of equality and inalienable rights, the special task has fallen to uphold the universalism of a people whose history has painfully taught it the disastrous consequences of narrower views. The American Jewish community possesses, if not a mission, then certainly a calling, a vocation, to stress to all men that the redemption has not yet come, that it lies far in the future, and that the dark present can be made lighter only insofar as it is drawn toward the luminous vision of the messianic ideal. Our existence as American Jews is tangible evidence that the God of Israel dwells not in space but in time, in history and in hope, that no mountaintop and no land anywhere can fully contain Him.

America is not Zion. The State of Israel is not Zion. Zion is a messianic symbol of complete fulfillment at the end of time. It is only in the end of days that the prophet's vision will be realized: "From Zion shall go forth the law and the Word of the Lord from Jerusalem."

The vocation of the Jewish people everywhere is to build Zion, not alone the earthly Zion—though we must certainly build that too—but the Zion of prophetic promise. This we must do together, I believe, Jews in America and Jews in Israel. We must do it for the sake of Israel the State, for the sake of Israel the people, and indeed for the blessing of all mankind.

NOTES

1. Theodor Herzl, *The Jewish State* (New York: American Zionist Emergency Council, 1946), pp. 76, 77, 123 (emphasis added).
2. *Proceedings of the Union of American Hebrew Congregations,* V (1898–1903), 4002.

Becoming a Friend to Myself:

With a Little Help from Sigmund Freud, Erich Fromm, and Martin Buber

ROBERT L. KATZ

My subject is self-esteem. I propose to define it and to consider with you some contributions of psychology and Judaism to what it means and how it is attained. In this Centennial lecture on so broad and almost presumptuous a theme, I aim to offer a running commentary on some old and some new perspectives on a task that faces us all. The search for self-esteem is a universal one, insistent, inescapable, without end. What we seek is meaning and significance in our human situation. To put it less philosophically, we are concerned about our worth. What do we really think about ourselves? Are we strangers, enemies, or friends to that self which is our unshakable companion.

Psychology helps us frame the question, suggests the issues, and points to the necessary conditions for a reasonably successful search. So often Judaism deals with the same issues, however different the language and the style. But going beyond the domain of science, beyond the techniques of the therapeutic art, religion calls us again and again to consider some truths about man which are rooted in the religious experience. Religion neither seeks nor requires the approval

Dr. Robert L. Katz is Joseph and Helen Regenstein Professor of Religion, Ethics and Human Relations.

of science. At the same time the relevance of religious truths often becomes clearer to us when we permit ourselves to confront the issues as formulated in the terms used by our secular colleagues.

We are driven back to reflect on older sources when we encounter a Freud, a Buber, or a Fromm. For me this encounter has made Judaism more coherent, more personal, and more precious. How important is it that these men be conventionally pious? That they formally identify with the institutions of Judaism? That they be "believers"? I count them as my friends and my teachers, and I stand in their debt as a man, as a Jew, and as a rabbi. They have helped me to become a friend to myself. Without them I might have missed or neglected some dimensions of Judaism and never attained an adequate sense of my own worth as a person.

To begin, what does it mean to be a friend to oneself? It means having a reasonably good regard for oneself, a sense of personal worth, of self-acceptance. It is the opposite of being indifferent or hostile to oneself. We expect friends to respect and cherish us. One who is not a friend to himself, rejects and resents himself. Ultimately he can become his own executioner, surrendering every trace of regard for himself as he is, destroying himself out of disgust with his failure to become what he dreamed he should have become. Self-esteem is, then, one of the most fundamental life-tasks of every man.

The validated research of psychologists and psychiatrists informs us that many people actually have less self-esteem than they are aware of. This is not a matter of innate modesty, an appropriate hedge about possible hubris. Low self-esteem is a state of mind and feeling which subtly shapes the quality of our day-by-day life, robbing us of zest and making us feel slightly troubled and mildly disappointed. Some of this pale, shadowy sense of guilt may be realistic. It is deserved, and it should be confronted and mastered by changing our behavior and accepting moral responsibility. But there is a sense in which this fluctuating, elusive sense of malaise has to do more with our experience of ourselves than with our failures as brothers, sisters, and citizens. We are not really sure we want ourselves as friends. Do I really enjoy being "me"? We now see that we are dealing not just with friendship but with the question of happiness, the joy of being and the joy of my being—me.

After a sermon dealing with the general theme of "happiness," a congregant came up to me and said, with just a trace of pride, "I am not all that unhappy." I thought then and I think now, even more confidently, that she was settling for awfully little. Her statement called to mind Thoreau's observation that men live lives of quiet desperation. We are all too familiar with those who are vociferously and hysterically unhappy, but what of those who are quietly, yes, humbly, desperate? They are not hopelessly and completely unhappy. They are just mildly miserable, and they feel they have no cause for complaint. They are quiet because they do not dream that there could be anything else for them. They live with themselves and find their lives flat and untouched by excitement or enthusiasm.

In the Mishna, in the Ethics of the Fathers, the question is asked: "Who is a rich man?" The answer given is: "The rich man is one who rejoices in his own portion." But you might say that only a fool would be content with what he has. That is not the American way. Such a person might also be naive or egocentric. Should he not aspire to more than just his "portion"? If you insist on the achievement syndrome, note that the Mishna does not forbid anyone from adding to his portion. It is the enjoyment that the Mishna stresses, the sense of contentment with oneself, with one's achievements and with one's potentialities.

Is the entire question of self-esteem or happiness a luxury that we have no right to look for in a world that is filled with so much pain? How can we justify something as personal as the quest for private satisfaction or contentment when all around us men betray each other, degrade, violate, and exploit their brothers? There are higher priorities than peace of mind. Society has more urgent needs, and this concern with inner states of being deflects our attention from the pathology of our cities and from many violations of the basic rights of man. Should we not cast our portion with those who struggle for sheer survival?

There is an issue here only for those who would give exclusive attention to their private needs. We may have even more energy and love for others when we confront our own needs and, having gained some respect for who and what we are, expand the circle of our love to include others. History has known not a few passionate revolutionaries whose impulse to tear down the establishment has not been balanced with real care for those they were dedicated to redeem. Self-esteem for individuals is both a private and a communal value. When it is genuine, it is not self-regarding to the exclusion of others. It often leads to social involvement. Those who think of it as an end in itself confuse self-respect with self-indulgence.

We who are formally identified with religious institutions often exemplify a self-righteousness which belies our own commitment to *hesed* (lovingkindness). I shall shortly invite Freud, Fromm, and Buber to persuade you that love cannot begin anywhere else but in love of self. The theological basis for this truth about man is foreshadowed in the opening chapter of Genesis. Man is created in the image, or model, of God—he is therefore a bearer of the Divine and deserving of that love which is part of the utlimate reality which is love of God.

Having dealt briefly with the issue of peace of mind versus social conscience, we now turn to consider why there is any need to become better friends with ourselves. I would propose a test to determine whether we are sufficiently at peace with ourselves and with our place in the world. The test involves no exploration of the unconscious, no uncovering of our projections, no exposing of our paranoid ideation. Can you say these words—taken from our prayer book— fully and without reservation: "Blessed are thou, our Lord our God"? Can you say it and really mean it? Is your life blessed as you perceive it and as you experience it? Can you say with the Psalmist, "Oh Lord, open Thou my lips and my mouth shall declare Thy praise"? What a magnificent, dramatic expression of gratitude for the pure joy of being alive! Can you join me in saying, "Happy are they who dwell in Thy house; they shall continually praise Thee"? This is religious, theological language for the phenomenon which in psychology goes by the name of self-esteem. Do I equate psychology and theology? For me the human experience is the more important, but psychological terms afford me a handle to grasp the meaning of the religious symbols and appreciate their rich evocations. I require both the text, which is religion, and the commentary, which for me have been the sciences of man. Ultimately I must check both the text and the commentary against my own experience, the sense of who

I am and the confrontation of what is true of me and what represents the way I feel about myself.

We know for a fact that many of us need all the help we can get because a common tendency is to deprecate the worth of the self and to fantasize that others enjoy being themselves more than we enjoy being ourselves. It is a psychological finding that the most common posture is to say, "You're OK; I'm not OK." This observation, as phrased by the psychiatrist Thomas Harris, is not earth-shaking in content or particularly elegant in style, but it makes the issue plain and clear. Why this disposition—all too common—to deprecate ourselves? Psychoanalysts explain it in terms of the experience of childhood, when we were small and dependent, surrounded by powerful parents and older siblings who towered over us. Traces of that early memory may influence our present feelings about ourselves, even after we mature to our full powers. Long after we have become complete equals, a tendency may persist to make comparisons unfavorable to us, as if we were still children who can only fantasize what it must be like to be a full adult and to possess those powers and privileges.

For some social scientists, self-esteem is a loose concept which does not point to any identifiable reality. You cannot measure self-esteem, they say, because there simply is no general state of mind or being. There are only derivatives and reactions to particular situations. Happiness is a function of a concrete experience; no one is simply "happy." Self-esteem is a sometime, contingent thing. If you get a raise or a bonus, your self-esteem goes up. If you are dismissed from your job, your self-esteem sinks. If you are honored or, more fortunately, loved, you feel contented. If your children are successful or, more modestly, if they stay out of trouble, you feel some contentment with your portion. What some people question is the existence of some persistent, stable, solid sense of self-esteem which endures through the vicissitudes of experience in the family or on the job.

I take the position of my teachers, Freud, Fromm, and Buber, that there is an essential self, an enduring perception of the self, a core of sameness. Peace of mind is a reflection of this inner core. Fluctuations of mood aside, we do have a fairly consistent image of ourselves. Call it a baseline, if you will. We move up and down from it as

different situations call forth different reactions, but there is an irreducible quantity of selfness, and it is with this self-experience that
we are concerned.

It is an exercise in pure chutzpah (nerve plus pride) for me to
attempt to do justice to the insights of my psychological and religious
masters within the limits of a single lecture. If I have selected some
insights and neglected others, recall that, as my lecture topic indicates, I speak for myself and, inescapably, about myself. My responses
to these masters of the soul stand out on their own ground. I shall at
least have introduced you to three of my teachers, all of them Jews,
all of them lights along my own road to becoming a friend to myself.

Of the three, Erich Fromm, is alive, continuing to write, to lecture,
and to speak out on matters of private and public conscience. Fromm
was our guest scholar-in-residence some twenty years ago, and our
alumni continue to attest to the power of his teachings. While I
know Fromm and had the privilege of hearing Buber lecture on the
occasion of his visit to the University of Michigan in 1957, I know
Freud only from my studies with those who worked directly with him
or with his original students and from my own reading of his works.

Freud was the least Jewish and the least molded by the sources of
Judaism. Like Heine, he was an infidel Jew. He presented himself as
one who was emancipated form the chains of illusion. It is fascinating
that a scientist so proud of his personal liberation from religion should
have been engrossed in the study of religious phenomena, writing books
like *Moses and Monotheism* and *The Future of an Illusion* and
essays like "Obsessive Acts and Religious Practices." He felt identified
with Jews, and in his writing on humor and in his letters he revealed
himself as the cultural Jew par excellence. To the B'nai B'rith of
Vienna he wrote: "You were a great help to me when the world was
against me; you gave me an audience and I felt with you a clean,
clear, pure sense of inner identification." Freud believed that he could
successfully take the role of solitary opposition to the establishment
because this was a role familiar to the Jew.

One of his close friends was a Swiss pastor named Oskar Pfister.
In a letter dated October 9, 1918 in which Freud incidentally re-
ferred to the "beauty of religion" having no place in psychoanalysis,
the founder of psychoanalysis asked his friend, with tongue in cheek,

"how comes it that none of the godly ever devised psychoanalysis and that one had to wait for a godless Jew?" Pfister's reply was a masterpiece. On the one hand he chides Freud for not being more of a Jew, and then, reciprocating Freud's irony, suggests that he cannot really be godless since, in the words of John (4:16), he who fights for the freeing of love "dwelleth in God."

Freud identified with Jochanan ben Zakkai, who carried on the teaching of Torah at the academy of Jabneh, outside Jerusalem, after the victory of the Romans over the Jews. Leaving Nazi-occupied Vienna and going into exile in England, he was a modern Jochanan ben Zakkai, preserving the discoveries of psychoanalysis. Freud identified especially with Moses, the emancipator and law-giver. Traveling to Rome to stand before Michelangelo's statue of Moses had unusual meaning for the master therapist, convinced as he was that it was his destiny to liberate the psyche of man from the tyranny of unreason.

What, then, does Freud offer us in our quest for self-esteem? It was a revolutionary psychology Freud gave us, and our thinking about ourselves can never again be the same. It was not that he discovered something totally new. What he did was confirm the profound insights of poets and novelists, ground them in the real data of human experience, and formulate them into an intelligible, coherent system.

Freud complained that everywhere he was being asked to provide a faith. It was a task for which he was not equipped. He did have faith in the powers of the human personality to come up with a synthesis, once a proper job of analysis was done. He aimed to strip off the layers of illusion, confident that the human mind could then cope with reality. His modest goal, one that required months and years of psychological investigation, was to establish a procedure to free up the energies of the patient, who could then cope independently with the everyday variety of unhappiness. While Freud considered himself a scientist more than a therapist, and denied the intention of being a teacher of humanity, the end result of his study of the psyche was to make it possible for people to work through their blocks to self-esteem and to gain or regain a sense of confidence in their own powers.

His genius lay in helping us understand the way we shape our own destiny. He once wrote that when we are burdened and discontented with ourselves, it is usually not because something has entered into us from the outside and frustrated us in our search for personal meaning and worth, but because it is we ourselves who withdraw our energies from the work we must do. We interfere with our own use of our potential powers.

What so many of us suffer from is not delusions of grandeur but delusions of inadequacy. Honest appraisal of ourselves makes it possible for us to move toward greater self-respect. To make an honest appraisal is no simplistic maneuver, for we often disguise our strengths and rationalize our weaknesses in stubborn and often clever patterns of self-frustration. But Freud insisted that nothing less than total honesty could undo our defenses and expose the core from which self-esteem can grow.

It is paradoxical that Freud could be at one with Copernicus and Darwin in disabusing mankind of some of its most cherished illusions and at the same time could offer a vision of hope for rational man, who can achieve considerable power over his unconscious. Copernicus dealt man a cosmic blow to his pride, proving to him that his earth is not the center of the universe. The biological blow came from Darwin. But Freud, who dealt man the psychological blow by recognizing the power of the unconscious, provided at the same time the vision of man liberated from the total domination of his unconscious.

While much of Freud has already been assimilated into our culture, it is not always recognized that far from being pessimistic or cynical, as he is commonly pictured, he offers a perspective on man that is open-ended. All too often we take the insights of Freud, pure or diluted, and use them aggressively against others and against ourselves. We are not what we pretend to be, and such affection as we may have for ourselves and for others is, we say, only the surface beneath which we hide our primitive lust and our jealousy. In certain philosophic asides Freud seemed persuaded that man is wolf to man. But Freud the scientist made us aware of the immense resources we have for coping, controlling, and sublimating our basic energies. Freud actually restores our confidence in ourselves and in our power to take over and manage successfully large sectors of our private experience which we have been all too ready to surrender as helpless victims. If a victim typically loses his self-respect, if ever he had it, the man who sees himself as the agent of his own powers feels a justified pride in who he is and what he can accomplish. Freud's basic method of extending the frontiers of self-awareness is fundamentally constructive. The fact that self-awareness is vastly difficult to attain in some cases, and that it requires constant monitoring, is also part of the reality that Freud taught us to recognize and to live with.

Freud believed, along with the classic philosophers, that reason can liberate man. He considered himself one of the liberators. Powerful as instincts may be, it is possible for man to master them, if, and this is a monumental if, he has insight into their power. Instead of being the rider of a runaway horse, man's ego can control the reins and guide the horse to go the way that he, the rider, chooses. Freud should be given an honored place among those who have restored to us our faith in human capacities. He taught us to recognize that we are permitting ourselves to become "victims," often of the blind instinctual forces within us, that we can modify the pattern and become the agents of our own destiny. We lack the full power over our lives to achieve the childhood dreams of omnipotence, but we can, Freud suggests, achieve a sense of self-mastery. It is a source of dignity that makes us feel the most profound respect for what we are and what we have been able to achieve, in the face of a bleak and harsh environment.

Freud's more philosophical essay, *Civilization and Its Discontents* contains the interesting speculation that someday we shall have a society more conducive to human fulfillment. Freud has something of the spirit of the Hebrew prophets when he suggests that the structure of society, as presently organized, defeats the genuine fulfillment of man. Erich Fromm, of course, developed this concept more articulately and passionately than Freud, but it is interesting to note that Freud, too, placed part of the difficulty of the human condition on society and not on the individual. This offers, to be sure, no immediate consolation to the individual concerned with securing and maintaining his self-esteem.

Freud was dinstinctively a psychologist, an expert in the changing moods of the individual, a diagnostician of the ailments of the soul.

If he has anything at all to teach us about self-esteem, it is that, more often than not, we suffer from unnecessary guilt sometimes created by our own fantasies and sometimes encouraged by well-meaning but misguided parents. Such feelings of guilt and inadequacy corrode the precious sense of personal well-being and rob us of what might have been a natural and easy zest in the use of our own energies.

Freud taught us that we do not have objective knowledge about ourselves. We do not see ourselves for what we really are because our feelings are enmeshed with the feelings and perceptions of our parents. We do not experience ourselves as separate and independent persons. The boundaries between the self and the parental family are fuzzy and shifting. Because we lack this sense of self, much of what we experience as our own is really our identification with the experience of our parental families. We often do not know how to distinguish between what we feel and what we have taken over second-hand from our childhood experience. Self-esteem, Freud would say, grows out of a sense of one's experience of himself as an independent person, no longer embedded in family experience. In other words, we have swallowed some of the feelings, perceptions, and demands of our parents without really having chewed them and made them our own. A more technical term for this image, taken from Fritz Perls, is "internalization." Freud meant simply that we have allowed ourselves to feel guilty and unworthy because we have never really looked at ourselves objectively and given ourselves a chance to work at becoming what we really are. The precondition for genuine self-esteem is detachment from the powerful figures of our childhood. We can then decide what our standards and expectations can reasonably be and judge for ourselves whether we have made sufficient progress toward goals we have freely chosen. But if the goals are not openly, honestly, and independently chosen but are, instead, picked up uncritically and blindly from others, as an unoriginal and passive commitment, made without awareness, then we can come to grief. The sensation of "non-goodness"—I would not go so far as to say "evil" or self-disgust—derives from the fact that we have not chosen . . . ourselves.

How does one liberate himself from such feelings of guilt and become a friend to himself? Not by rejecting parents and teachers. Much of what they have given us is true and realistic. Once having achieved autonomy, it is likely that we will choose many of the values of those whose love was so critical for us in our development as persons. Freud suggests that we must be active choosers, autonomous and self-directed. If we continue to be critical of ourselves, the criticism will be more friendly. We shall not belabor ourselves, Freud seems to imply, if it is our own expectations we have not fully met rather than expectations absorbed in childhood when we needed the love and approval of the parents. Without them we were helpless. But now as adults—no longer weak and vulnerable—we can be more trusting of our own powers and our own judgments.

We turn now to Erich Fromm, a contemporary psychoanalyst, whose books on psychology, religion, and social problems have been widely read. Happily, Fromm is alive and creative, spending most of each year in Mexico City, raising his voice from time to time in defense of the rights of man. He was twice scholar-in-residence here on our campus, and many of us remember him as a teacher and a friend. Most of his books deal with self-esteem, and one of them, *Man for Himself,* is a profound psycho-religio justification of man's right and duty to have self-respect. Fromm is not a formally believing Jew, but he has been a consistent student and exponent of Jewish ideals. He can be described as a humanist, but in sympathy and approach he is closely associated with Jewish sources.

Fromm received an excellent Jewish education in Frankfurt and throughout his career has maintained close contact with Jewish religious literature. He has expounded the Bible as well as the Talmud and the Midrash. With forgivable pride he indicates that some of the translations he provides are his own work.

By his training, his moral philosophy, and his constant concern with contemporary ethical issues, he is much more the teacher and the preacher than was Freud. While the founder of psychoanalysis was Jewish in his identifications, it is Fromm, the informed Jew and the passionate social critic, whose message was shaped more forcefully by the teachings of Judaism.

What was only incidentally alluded to in the writings of Freud—namely, that society itself must be transformed before individuals can live fully—is a dominant motif in the life and prolific work of Erich Fromm. Of some comfort to those of us who have wondered, at times, about the pain of adjustment to society and institutions is Fromm's observation that the only really healthy people in our society are the neurotics. We are so accustomed to the term "neurotic" as a pejorative term that it comes as some surprise to find it used almost eulogistically. Fromm should not be taken too literally. He has much to say about the inner changes that it is possible and necessary to make with therapy and education even while struggling to reform a society that is often immoral.

Fromm says we often give in too soon to the demands of an insane society. We adjust too quickly, with too little protest, to the dehumanizing pressures of the world. We settle for too little, too soon. Fromm obviously has little patience with the counselors and therapists who would ease our way into a comfortable conformity. Fromm sees us exhausting ourselves, tense, weary, and dull, running about to conform to changing norms, rarely pausing to determine for ourselves what it is that we really need.

There is a suspicion that self-esteem, like self-love, is something indulgent. It appears as a turning inward to care for oneself, to the exclusion of anyone else.

Fromm addresses himself to this issue and reminds us that self-love is the necessary basis for our love of others. We are so conditioned to suspect self-love that we consider it immoral, as objectionable as self-worship. Love of others seems good and proper; love of self is childish, improper if not antisocial.

Fromm observes that when we talk of self-love, we often talk about narcissism. We fail to distinguish between honest regard for oneself, says Fromm, and that preoccupation with oneself that really reflects unresolved doubts we continue to have about whether or not we deserve respect. Narcissism reflects self-doubt, self-love reflects acceptance of oneself, tolerant and even affectionate, recognizing one's deficiencies and lapses but having, in spite of this honest self-knowledge, a stable sense of well-being and a confidence about who we are and what we are doing. The narcissist tends to be frantic, constantly trying to reassure himself that he is likable.

What, then, are we to do, until the day when the more humane, civilized society comes? Fromm, who was deeply influenced by Marx as well as by Freud, never ceases to write about the pathology of our society, but at the same time he gives us insights about what we can do in shorter-range, more personal terms.

First, Erich Fromm releases us from whatever guilt we may have about even attempting to love ourselves. Fromm quotes the biblical text, "Thou shalt love thy neighbor as thyself" and indicates that love for others is possible only when we have succeeded in gaining our own regard for ourselves. It is the preconditon for social relations. It is anything but a diversion of feeling back into the self or a containment of energy that ought to be going from me to you. Self-love is not an indulgence—it is a requirement. In religious language—which Fromm finds congenial—it is a commandment.

Second, Fromm informs us that self-love is predicated on emotional independence. It is based on use of our own powers. For Fromm, this involves leaving the Garden of Eden. We have to abandon the child-like existence where we have no responsibilities or challenges, no autonomy and no dignity. Fromm uses the biblical image of the Garden of Eden to symbolize the parental family. We come of age when we individuate, when we become individuals, and this is not possible when our own lives are embedded in the lives of the powerful people upon whom we were totally dependent as children. For Fromm, as for all psychoanalysts, self-love becomes possible when the individual achieves a center of gravity within himself. So long as we are dependent upon the approval of others, we are tied symbiotically to them and our self-love is always vulnerable.

Fromm sees us putting ourselves down by repetitive confessions of guilt and inadequacy. We keep apologizing for our failures, lamenting the promises we have not kept, bemoaning our fate, regretting the compromises we agreed to. The forms may change, but the consistent note is regret for past mistakes. In several of his books, Fromm quotes from one of his favorite Hasidic teachings: "To have sinned or not to have sinned—what does it profit us in heaven? In the time I am brooding on this, I could be stringing pearls for the joy of heaven." Note how this passage captures so well the therapeutic philosophy of Fromm. As a rabbi, I am gratified that our religion informs Fromm's views so vividly.

One concluding thought from our teacher, Erich Fromm. It has to do with our feeling about people in general as well as about ourselves as persons. Fromm is struck by the fact that we are so quick to say that basically "people are corrupt" or that "human nature is no good"! In religious language this is the idea of "original sin"—the "natural" state of man. Why is this dismal view of human nature so widespread? Fromm explains that it provides us with the perfect cop-out. If human nature is evil and corruptible, then why should I expect anything more from myself? If I can be cynical about the future of mankind, I can be cynical about myself and my own worth.

To become friends to ourselves, we begin by giving up the rationalization that human nature is hopelessly corrupt and we start working on our own potentialities. This is Fromm—essentially a man of hope and a Jew who is in love with life.

And, now to the third of my teachers, to Martin Buber, the truly Renaissance man of contemporary Jewry. He died just eleven years ago, a poet, theologian, translator, educator, and an exponent of Hasidism, better known, at least in the Diaspora, by Christians than by Jews. He was, of course, still the most "Jewish" of the triad of teachers we are discussing. His major opus, *I and Thou,* has entered into the thinking of wide circles of theologians, educators, and psychologists.

Like Fromm, Buber said that too often we experience ourselves as commodities in a society of things. His term for that kind of self was an "it." While it is often necessary for us to function as if we were an "it," what gives most meaning to our lives is the fact that we are a "thou," a subject and not an object. As a "thou," we have an existential sense of self-esteem, of irreducible personal dignity.

We turn to some of Buber's insights and observations that are more immediately applicable to our theme, deriving as they do from Buber's existential philosophy.

The theme in Buber most closely related to the issue of our feelings about ourselves is his concept of guilt. Buber was concerned, as is Fromm, with guilt as a part of the human condition. To enjoy genuine self-esteem, one must determine what it is that he is responsible for and then he must actively meet that responsibility. Unlike neurotic guilt, the feelings of unworth deriving from certain accidents and influences of our childhood when we lived under the shadow of our parents and obeyed their wishes out of a mixture of love and fear, there is, says Buber, actual and real guilt which requires the therapy of action. If we feel that we are unworthy because we have neglected a certain sense of duty or of call within us, we deserve that feeling. Buber does not rule out the possibility that some of us suffer from the wrong kind of guilt, from an uncritically swallowed judgment of our parents leading us to feel that we have done something wrong when, in fact, there is no objective basis in our actual behavior for that feeling. That kind of guilt calls for psychological treatment. But Buber's concern is with what he calls our "existential guilt." To dull that sense of guilt, to desensitize ourselves to that feeling of being unworthy, is to dehumanize ourselves. It is equivalent to a moral lobotomy.

For Buber, Adam's experience in the Garden of Eden reflected his attempt to escape from his humanness and from the call of his real existence. When God calls to Adam and asks him, "Where are you?", Adam attempts to hide. Following the Hasidic interpretation, Buber explains that it is a model for man attempting to hide from his "call," an objective actual fact of his life, reflecting his own nature as the bearer of the Divine image. The wisdom of the religious sources, which Buber has reclaimed for us, suggests that much of our unhappiness is earned, for we do have a conscience which troubles our sleep and which demands a response and a decision from us. To gain or regain our self-esteem we can do no less than listen to the still, small voice of conscience.

The most practical response to that call is found in our meetings with our fellow men. When we truly engage in dialogue with our fellow man, we begin really to live. When we become fully present to another, we become more fully present to ourselves. I am oversimplifying Buber in stating that in such a meeting, another presence is also felt, because God is experienced in the in-between, in the meeting-ground that is common to the two persons. It is at such times, says Buber, that the heavenly bread of self-experience is passed from one to the other. When two people meet, it is as though they bowed to each other, each acknowledging the "thou" in the other.

Buber infrequently speaks of God, but belief in God suffuses and shapes his thinking about man. Buber wrote: "A man can ward off with all his strength the belief that God is there and then he can taste him in the strict sacrament of dialogue." Buber would have us believe that this language describes us as we really are and as we might be. Buber believes that we are more than psychological precipitates of a family process. We are also part of the structure of the world, and the place we have in that world makes demands on us from which there can be no escape. In fact it is only by standing and confronting these demands that we can hope to achieve a sense of personal dignity and genuine peace of mind. Guilt is therefore not something to be dissolved or reduced. It is to be lived with and to be confronted as part of a continuous response to being human.

One brilliant phrase of Buber's has impressed me. It has brought home to me personally the special meaning of his teachings about self-esteem. Buber speaks of the "shudder of identity." What he means by this phrase is that at one time or another, in our thinking about ourselves and in our reflecting about our past and our future, we are caught by a sudden perception of who we are. We recognize, in a single, vivid, moment, that the person we are today and the person we once were are the very same person. If we missed an opportunity in the past, we are the same person who is at this moment missing an opportunity to repair an injury, to do what we must do. It makes us shudder because now we have a sense of closure about our own identity. Yesterday glides into the present moment; we are indivisible from what we once were. We are the same, and unless we act now we are inevitably going to repeat the kind of mistake we made in the past. There is a continuity to our experience. If we were guilty once before, we are guilty now. Nothing of the essential core of ourselves has changed. We stand the perpetual risk of imagining that we are different from what we were in the past, and it is with no small sense of shock, according to Buber, that we reognize that we are essentially the same and that our task remains unaltered and undiminished in its pressure on us.

Is this "shudder of identity" something to welcome or relish? It will not make us feel immediately more comfortable with ourselves, but it does give a certain cohesion to the self. It makes us better acquainted with the flow of experience that we call our own careers.

On the basis of that confrontation with self, we can move to higher levels of self-esteem.

What impressed me as I reviewed some highlights in the thinking of Freud, Fromm, and Buber, particularly as they touched on the search we all take for self-esteem, is a concern with the inner life of the individual. Perhaps we consider this emphasis on inner or self-experiences to be something natural and familiar, but even the familiar becomes unknown simply because it is so close at hand. How many of us, for example, take prayer seriously and experience it freshly and meaningfully each time we speak the well-known phrases and doxologies? Valuable as religious practices and teachings are for inner life, their usefulness remains something potential, untapped, and unappreciated. The psychologists, perhaps because they use the scientific language, the secular jargon, rather than the poetico-religious imagery, can help us become more responsive to insights in our religious tradition, long latent and unused. They provide a commentary on the text, not revelatory or radical, but evocative and stimulating.

I am not saying that our religious tradition anticipated every insight of dynamic psychology or that Judaism is the only authentic guide to self-esteem. My point is that these psychological teachers help us recover what may have been lost to us, because we live in a different thought-world and speak and read the language of the scientist.

Only a few examples need to be given. They simply call attention to the concern of Judaism for the individual. The saying of Hillel is the most familiar. If I am not for myself, who is for me? Paraphrasing this in the terms of this lecture, if I am not a friend to myself, who then will be a friend to me? And if I am for myself exclusively, i.e., if I am narcissistically preoccupied with myself, then what do I amount to?

Consider also the statement that each person ought to go about with certain messages descriptive of himself. In one pocket, he should carry a slip of paper with the statement that God has made him but little lower than the angels. And in the other pocket, the second slip should remind him that man is but dust and ashes. Here is the balance, profoundly humanistic and starkly existential, which supports the structure of self-esteem. We are protected from self-degrading humility and from neurotic dreams of glory.

The Ethics of the Fathers contains this saying of a rabbi: "Do not be wicked in your own eyes." It says we ought to beware of a tendency to put ourselves down too often and too consistently. The psychologist might comment on the Mishnaic text and ask: Why this need to deprecate yourself? Against what model do you compare yourself so unfavorably? Maimonides made an interesting psychological commentary of his own. He said that if you continue to consider yourself totally wicked, then you will feel motivated to do nothing by way of repenting. You get yourself off the hook, because as a totally hopeless person, your lapses will be understood and few demands will be made on you.

There is a fascinating passage which holds that better is one hour of repentance and good works in this world than all of the life to come. What that means is that repentance is an active process of changing and that there is more human dignity in the process of growing and changing than there could possibly be in the passive, though blissful, residence in the world to come.

For me one of the most eloquent expressions of Judaism on the subject of man and his worth is found in the Yom Kippur liturgy when the rabbi faces the open ark and reads the prayer at the climax of the Ne'ilah service. The prayer speaks of the experience of being overwhelmed by the wonders of the universe and the thought of God's greatness. But it is the theme of man's superb endowment that marks the climax of the prayer—"had you not placed man at the very summit of creation . . ." The self-esteem we look for is not a pedestrian, lackluster concept of mental health as a least common denominator of well-adjusted, conforming, law-abiding citizens. In the religious view it moves us to heights. We come to esteem ourselves for what we are and for what we can become.

Moved as we may be by the words of religion or by the insights of the great doctors of the soul, Freud, Fromm, and Buber, the task of achieving self-esteem, of becoming friends to ourselves, involves a choice. It is the same choice spelled out in the words of Deuteronomy. "Behold, I set before thee life and death, the blessing and the curse; therefore choose life, that thou mayest live . . ."

As a Jew and as a man, I hope to choose life. I am grateful to all who have told me what the choice is and to those who have helped me appreciate my own responsibility in making that choice.

Jewish-Christian Relations in Our Time

SAMUEL SANDMEL

My assumption is that your interest is in the topic and not primarily in me, and yet I think that I ought to say a few things about myself so that you can discount whatever bias is inevitable in any presentation. My parents were Europeans; I am a first-generation American. They came to these shores fleeing from pogroms, which began with the ringing of church bells; one of my childhood memories is how my mother used to shiver whenever the church bells rang in the Roman Catholic neighborhood in which we lived. I am a rabbi; I have a Ph.D. degree, whatever that means, in New Testament. In the transition from the experience of parents in Europe to my own American experience, there is contained an epitome of what I want to discuss with you this evening.

Jewish-Christian relations is a topic of some delicacy, and the possibility of misunderstanding is omnipresent, and the challenge a bit arduous so to couch things that there is tolerably reasonable communication. One cannot in one lecture deal with everything; moreover, there are some areas in which, immodestly, I can lay claim to experience and competency, but some areas where I have only an acquaintance.

Dr. Samuel Sandmel is Distinguished Service Professor of Bible and Hellenistic Literature.

Thus, for example, my life has been largely that of an academician in an academic setting; my life has not been that of a businessman in the downtown community. Hence my perspective on the topic is inevitably shaped by the academic life.

In order to speak about Jewish-Christian relations today, I have to touch on the past, and to do so with what I am afraid will be an excess of brevity. Among the valid reasons for looking into the past is to find guideposts by which to measure how far we may have moved forward; by noting the unhappy situations long ago we may, by contrast, be able to assess what is valid for our own time.

The acute problem in Jewish-Christian relations derives from what is basic, that Christianity was born within Judaism. Jesus was a Jew; his immediate followers were Jews; that which brought them together was a Jewish purpose, but it was not too long before the movement ceased to be one of Jews and ceased to have a direct Jewish purpose. The movement spread beyond the borders of Judea. As is the case universally in movements which arise within an older movement, there was the inevitable need of the newer movement to justify its separation from its parent, that is, to set forth the bases on which it separated, and to give its evaluation of the issues on which it separated. One should reasonably expect from the younger movement a criticism of the older movement, with the possibility present that the criticism is partisan. The parent, on the other hand, may not react in the same focused way, and, indeed, may have been beset by quite a variety of concerns, only one of which was some new and possibly dissident movement. We inherit from the past, literature by Christians which focuses on Judaism. It sets forth Christian contentions. It sets them forth in what can objectively be described as aspersions of Jews and Judaism. The tone of such aspersions needs to be inquired into, for some of these aspersions include a bitterness which, when we meet it today, may upset us.

I would ask you to accept my report that in the literature of that bygone age, there was no tradition of Lord Chesterfield and his gentility! There is a tone of unrelieved animosity in the ancient Christian writings against Jews and Judaism, but that same tone characterizes Christian writings against the cornerstone of American education, the Greek classic tradition, and the hostility was even more unrestrained when a second-century Christian spoke about a fellow Christian with whom he disagreed. Relatively, the anti-Jewish tone is mild compared with that of a Christian attacking a fellow Christian. One must keep this factor of tone in mind if we are to have some perspective on why things took the shape they did.

The standpoint of Christianity, as a movement born within Judaism and admittedly Jewish in its roots, was this, that it regarded itself as the top rung of the ladder of God's revelation, which had begun with Abraham, and which reached its pinnacle with Jesus. While there were minor voices (which did not survive) that contended that Christianity had not originated in Judaism and owed no debt to it, such views were marginal and peripheral and quickly disappeared. Rather, the view became crystallized that Christianity was the highest form of Judaism. Christians were the true Israel of God. Christians had supplanted in God's favor the Jews who antecedently had had it; there were some Christians who went on to say that the Jews had clearly lost God's favor, and now that Christianity had come onto the scene, there was no excuse for Judaism to persist. The paradox that Christianity centered in Jews such as Jesus and Paul, and yet Jews seemed not to respond to the Christian message in the same way that Gentiles did, led to the contentions that Jews were blind, Jews were gratuitously hostile, and Jews were damned, and their religion a risreputable one.

From the Jewish side, we might be reasonably sure that compliment elicited compliment if only we had more surviving documents. We do not possess a legacy of Jewish anti-Christian literature of the same quantity as the Christian anti-Jewish literature. We have inherited only limited overtones, passing sentences, rather than rounded and well-constructed essays. The reason for the legacy of Christian anti-Jewish writing is that Christianity needed to find some basis itself for its having been born in Judaism and having departed, but Judaism did not feel the same need to define Christianity. One searches in vain in the ancient Rabbinic literature for some expression of a crystal-clear Jewish theological attitude to Christianity, analogous to the crystal-clear Christian theological attitude to Judaism. I am not suggesting that there were no Jewish counterparts to the Christian anti-Jewish writings; I am saying that if there were counterparts, they have not survived to our day. In a word, Jews and Judaism figure in Christian Scripture, but Christians and Christianity do not figure in Jewish Scripture.

The Christian documents speak of Jewish persecution of Christians. One who is something of a pedant would prefer that such statements read that there was Jewish violence, or, rather, violence on the part of some Jews against some Christians, and not persecution in an organized sense, this a product of directives from some established authority. In Acts of the Apostles (the account of the church after the time of Jesus), we read of sporadic outbursts on the part of Jews against Christians, followed by periods of peace in which the Christian community in Judea appeared to prosper and to grow, these followed by other acts of hostility, and thereafter again quiet and peacefulness.

Out of Christian theological views about Jews and Judaism there arose consequences for Jews throughout the Middle Ages and into modern times (depending on how we define modern times). These consequences included limitations, or prohibitions, respecting where Jews could live, limitations respecting the trades and occupation they could follow and the clothes they wore, an obligation to wear an identifying piece of cloth called the "Jew badge," instances of unrestrained, violent persecution that came from deputized authorities, carried out with some diligence by the state, which was under the influence or under the control of the church. There were other painful moments in medieval Jewish history, such as the invitation to Jews to become Christians or be deported. There were Jews who, to escape the cruelties, went through a nominal conversion and then were subjected to the courts of the Inquisition and by them treated with the same severity that was used on all people against whom allegations of deviation from fidelity were made. The record includes expulsions from this dukedom or that kingdom; it includes the "charters" that enabled a Jewish community to settle in some locality but limited the number of Jews allowed there, restricted the trades they were allowed to pursue, and specified even the limited number of marriages to be permitted.

Part of the record is in the realm of developed folklore: Jews have a peculiar odor; Jews utilize the blood of a Christian child, rather than wine, on Passover; Jews have an unusual adaptness at earning money;

Jews have a body of "arcana," of secret data, which they alone are privy to and which are carefully shielded from outside scrutiny.

Jews also developed a folklore: a gentile, a *goy,* a Christian, was distinguished by his physical force, for he was powerful, gifted with strong arms, while a Jew was weak A Christian relied on his physical force, a Jew on his intellect. I was reared under the influence of worthy, kindly parents. Yet their experience in Europe had conditioned them to the conclusion that a goy is a drunkard. The notion that there were sober Christians, or intelligent Christians, or high-minded Christians, did not occur to them in Europe because such Christians were outside their ken. They had attributed to Christians a relentless animosity against Jews; its proof was in the record of persecution, one example of which, in the early 1900s, brought my parents to these shores.

One more facet of background. Many of you know the name of Leo Baeck, rabbi from Germany, who chose to go into a concentration camp when he might have escaped, and he survived and ultimately taught here at Hebrew Union College a semester a year. He represented a kind of curious phenomenon in Germany, that of a Jew who wrote a number of essays on Christianity, Christian doctrines, and Christian contentions. In a sense, somebody like me is a successor to Leo Baeck. We will never understand Christian-Jewish relations in the United States if I do not point out some differences between his environment and mine. The scholarship that emerged from Germany in Baeck's time was quantitatively and qualitatively the best of the nineteenth century. That scholarship was independent, free, in a sense somewhat iconoclastic, having broken with inherited Christian tradition. But one says with the deepest regret that that scholarship was shot through and through with slurs against Jews and insults to Judaism. What somebody like Leo Braeck felt that he had to do, at least as he saw it, was to enter the arena and defend Judaism academically. He himself was not connected with any university. In 1892, a great German Jewish scholar had lamented that there was not a single chair in Judaism in any German university. In 1875, the year in which the College was founded, German Jews had created what they called the Advanced Institute for the Study of Judaism; the government stepped in and compelled the atuhorities to change the name to Teachers' Institute.

Now to the American contrast. I was on the faculty of Vanderbilt University before I came to Hebrew Union College. Today we take the appointments in Judaica in America for granted, possibly because we are not aware of their absence in the European past.

The difference between the German scene and the American scholarship in religion may be well epitomized in a personal incident. When I taught at Vanderbilt, there was on the faculty an American married to a lovely German woman, who was the niece of the foremost New Testament scholar of our time, Rudolf Bultmann. Professor Bultmann came to Vanderbilt to give a series of lectures, and inquiring about its faculty, he was told about me, and he misunderstood; he said to his nephew and his niece, as they reported it to me, "In Germany we would never have tolerated on the faculty of a Protestant Divinity School somebody married to a Jewess." When he was told that I was not only married to a Jewess but was a rabbi, his response was, "This is wonderful. In Germany we learned about Judaism from books, never from Jews."

The clue to comparing and contrasting the European scene and the open American society is the word "separate." There was in Europe a separation in languages. My parents did not use the language of the land where they were born. My father could speak it, and could read and write it, but my mother knew scarcely any of it. Again, when I was a little boy, I had to stay out of school on the Jewish New Year in order to go to synagogue, but after lunch—what did children do before there was radio or television?—my brothers and I went to a movie, and a truant officer picked me up, demanding to know why we weren't in school. My father was not allowed to go to the public school where he was born; I was compelled to, here where I was born. In an open society, one has experiences that never occur in a closed society.

The experiences in the Western open society have not always been affirmative, whether in my case or the case of many of you who sit here. There is a lingering strangeness, an enigmatic quality, that usually remains below the surface, arising from the mystery of the relationships of the Christian and Jewish communities to each other, often marked by a certain excessive awareness, a certain uneasiness which one struggles to keep out of the overtones of his conversation. Perhaps it does not extend as far as to suspicion, but perhaps at times it does. There is also the occasional untoward incident, or that painful slur that we Jews are quick to pick up, both when it is intended and when it is not. Yet we do pick it up, and indeed sometimes we are guilty of comparable slurs on Christians, because we sometimes are totally unaware that we are engaging in slurs.

How has a free society affected our relations with Christians? About what goes on in the business world downtown you will have to turn to someone else. I know a few overtones. There is the social situation wherein there are Jewish clubs and Jewish country clubs and there are either Gentile or Christian town clubs or country clubs. It has sometimes escaped my scrutiny of what there is Christian about a Christian club or Jewish about a Jewish club, but there are these social demarcations, and there are incidents.

Those of you who are in my age group will never get over the trauma of Hitler, even if you, like me, had never been in Europe until after World War II. I joined the Navy in World War II. I was a chaplain. Let me confess that I wanted to fight Hitler; in its wisdom the Navy sent me to the Southwest Pacific. I had by then already begun to work in New Testament. On entering the Navy, I was thrown into contact, first at Chaplain School, and then in the regular duties with Christian chaplains of many kinds, just as there were many kinds of Jewish chaplains. But how could any rabbi with any sensitivity fail to discover, to reverse the words of Shakespeare, the reality: Hath not a Christian eyes? Hath not a Christian hands, organs, dimensions, senses, affections, passions, fed with the same food, hurt with the same weapons, subject to the same diseases, healed by the same means, warmed and cooled by the same winter and summer, as a Jew is?

How, in an open society, in free associations, could one escape having some glimpse of the common humanity of all people?

Between the time I had begun studies in New Testament at Duke University before World War II, and when I completed the work for a Ph.D. after the war, six million Jews were killed in Europe. The only thing that happened to me was to be away from home, from my wife, to be frightened a few times by the Japanese. Others suffered horribly. I did not. I served; I learned.

I am a rabbi who works in New Testament. In Germany, I said earlier, there were no academic chairs. You are not interested in me personally, but you might be interested in how it happened that I taught at Vanderbilt. I was in student work at the University of North Carolina, which position I had wanted so that I could do a Ph.D. in Bible—that is, Old Testament. I drove ten miles to Duke University, a Methodist school, so as to enroll for a Ph.D. I was directed to the chairman of the department, who talked with me in a friendly way. He said, "We don't give a degree in Old Testament. How about doing it in New?" And after making the suggestion, this man went on to urge me. He mentioned an East European, Joseph Klausner, who had settled in modern-day Palestine, who had written on Jesus. He mentioned a British scholar, Claude G. Montefiore, who had written many works on Christianity, and he said, "Wouldn't it be wonderful if there were an American Jew who wrote in this field?"

I started studying. Very soon this gentleman, who was the son, the grandson, the great-grandson, the great-great-grandson of a line of Methodist ministers, concluded that he wanted to create a Chair of Jewish Studies at Duke. They did not want such chairs in Germany, but this American wanted it. Why? Because he had been a student indirectly of an American named George Foot Moore, a Presbyterian, who had written a book called *Judaism,* a book in two volumes, with a third volume of notes. All of us have daydreams about what we would like to have done—the Walter Mitty syndrome. My own Walter Mitty daydream is that I wish I had written the book that George Foot Moore wrote!

He preceded it by an essay in 1921 in the *Harvard Theological Review* called "Christian Writers on Judaism" wherein he gave the history of what Christians had written, and then paid attention to the work of some German scholars which I have alluded to.

Moore was not someone marked primarily by a compelling love for Jews or Judaism. He had that, but that was not what animated him. He was a free scholar whose concern was the truth, and therefore he had written his book. It influenced that professor at Duke, Harvie Branscomb. Branscomb subsequently established a Chair of Jewish

Studies at Duke, and, later becoming the Chancellor at Vanderbilt, established a Chair of Jewish Studies there, too; that's how I happened to teach at Vanderbilt. Now, that which did not happen in Germany happened in America.

If you were to look at the academic books in the field of New Testament before George Foot Moore and the books which came after he wrote, you would find the tone of the writing completely different.

Sporadically, in an imperfect world, I have come across scholarship, sometimes by Christians, sometimes by Jews, that contain slurs; this is rare today. The one time that I can recall being somewhat vividly upset by a passage in a book on early Christianity, wondering how this could have emerged from the American scene, I discovered that the author was a European who had moved here! No, American scholarship is remarkably free of what characterized the German scholarship of the nineteenth century.

As to the sociology of Christians and Jews (I have opinions that are no better than yours), and the ways in which individuals and committees react to each other, and the patterns of the established social norms which become liquidated only over the longest period of time —I have no great wisdom about them. My knowledge is of the academic world.

As to Vanderbilt, it was either the third or fourth Chair of Jewish Studies in the United States. Today the number is beyond counting. As to the academic world and Christian-Jewish relations in our time, it is not alone that George Foot Moore wrote his masterpiece of scholarship. It is that, very significantly the tone of Christian scholarship has altered from that in the Middle Ages. Then there were public disputations which Jews were compelled to participate in; then the object in the disputations was for each disputant to demolish his opponent if he could. There were scholars who compiled source books of "ammunition" for these unhappy enterprises. In our time there has arisen, among Jews and Christians, a common search for the truth, a common quest. Collaboration in academic enterprises by Jews and Christians is no longer a novelty. The free and equal exchange of information and opinion is inherently part of the American scene. These are things that we take for granted because we have been doing it long enough so that it does not make an impression on us.

Here in Cincinnati, if I am not mistaken about the date, we have been having a joint Thanksgiving service for about seventy-five years. I think we take it so for granted that, usually, we do not go to it. Something like this would be startling across the ocean.

Jews and Christians meet together in professional societies in the area of religion. In the Society of Biblical Literature, there have been four Jews who have been elected the Society's President; and if you will pardon the institutional pride, all have been professors at Hebrew Union College.

What is it that we Jews and Christians have learned? I think we have learned how to assess the ancient hostilities I think, in part, we have learned the counter-measures that are necessary to prevent the hostilities from being resurrected in our time, and to prevent their being indiscriminately utilized by the "sick" of our time. I think we Jews have learned that there is more to Christian documents than just the motif of the hostility to Jews. True, the hostility is there, but that is, in context, only one theme, and Christian scholars are just as much aware of it as Jews. How Christians will cope with that motif is their problem—but that there are efforts to cope with it I can attest to. The literature that has emerged from Christians in this area includes books that set forth, calmly and academically, the facts, free from partisanship, about the nature of Judaism. In the past year a Roman Catholic woman, Rosemary Ruether, has written a book called *Faith and Fratricide,* which is a profound inquiry into the nature of the anti-Jewish sentiment in ancient Christianity. It is a book of the utmost candor and truth, marked by the most elevated human sympathy that one could hope for.

Have we been able to come to some religious understanding? Religious comprehension of each other, perhaps, but religious agreement, no. In the first place, Christians are so divided, and Jews are so divided, that neither community is able to come to its own full unity, and therefore I do not think that we need to expect any agreement.

One thing we have indeed learned: to rise above words and phrases. It is a reality that often the convictions of Christians are expressed in one way and the convictions of Jews expressed in a different way, and yet these convictions are similar or identical or at least congruent. When we have penetrated below the surface, we have found that there the distinctions are less acute than the surface would suggest. Moreover, when we bring into full context the forces beyond Judaism and Christianity, we are much closer to each other than we ever dreamed we were.

I do not think there is much prospect that the Jews will share in the traditional view of the divinity of Jesus, and I do not think that ordinary Christians are going to share in the Jewish rejection of the divinity of Jesus, but I do think that the issue is not as divisive as once it was. We are able to talk about it with each other and able to understand, each the position of the other. If hostility and suspicion and disparagement give way to some sympathy, to some desire to understand, and some capacity to appreciate, then we will have realized the fullest measure of what the modern age can supply

Last, I want to run the risk of speaking about an item that is fraught with tension. Let me introduce it this way. It is a reality that the membership of the Nazi party was recruited from Christian circles. Most of us Jews are somewhat reluctant to confront the fact that Nazism was as anti-Christianity as it was anti-Judaism. I would hope that we Jews for whom Hitler remains a trauma, as I confess he does for me, will be able to discriminate between Nazis and Christians. In the Middle Ages, when Christians persecuted us, what they said to us was, "If you don't join us, we are going to drive you out of this country. Won't you please join us?" These Christians were opaque; they were cruel; they were issuing to us an invitation we did not want to accept. But all we had to do to be free of persecution was to accept the inivtation. That was not the case with the Nazis. The Nazis said, "You are a Jew and we are going to kill you, and our definition of a Jew is somebody who had one Jewish grandfather."

Let us not confuse Christians with Nazis. If there is anything that is unusual in the nineteenth century, it is that Christianity, which had been the persecutor, often became the defender of Jews. The pogroms in Damascus in 1842, the infamous Mortara affair in the 1850s, the pogroms in the 1880s, their renewal in the 1900s, elicited from Christian dignitaries expressions of sympathy that are exactly the opposite of the hostility of the Middle Ages.

I would be reluctant for us to gloss over some realities which exist. In both communities there are extremists. I have a small collection of books by Jews that are animated with the most unreserved hatred of or contempt for Christians, and I am aware that in the southwestern part of the United States there have emerged comparable books from Christians about Jews and Judaism, so that I am not stating that we have reached Utopia. I am only saying that the American experience has brought it about that Jews and Christians have come into a relationship that is quite different from anything previous in history. While there is some similarity in Holland and in Britain, the similarities there are not to the same degree; they are not to the same extent of penetration that characterizes the relations of American Jews and American Christians. The chief distinctiveness in the United States is in the realm of the everyday life of everyday people. Elsewhere, and previous to the founding of America, Jews and Christians were physically separated from each other, both by physical walls and by laws which, in effect, made them into distinct communities. They did not sit side by side in mandatory public schools, and their parents did not encounter each other in areas such as the PTA, or in business associations, or in communal endeavors, as is reflected in our daily pursuits today. Jews and Christians in the United States have become acquainted with each other on a personal basis in a way that has been unique in time, and unique in depth and integrity.

Where do we move from here? Somebody like me, I think, has two concerns as a rabbi. One is the welfare, the safety, of Jews. Another concern is that our religious tradition, so precious to me, be viably transmitted. I see nothing in these concerns that contradicts my wish accurately to understand Christianity, to understand it sympathetically, to appreciate it at its best, and to portray it to my fellow Jews on this or that occasion with the fullest responsibility. I should want to have the capacity to speak and write about Christianity in the same way in which I should wish Christians to write about Jews and Judaism.

The Biblical Base of Western Democracy:

The Record and the Prospects

HERBERT C. BRICHTO

The Great Pyramid at Gizeh, the pyramid of Cheops, rises from its base, which covers upwards of thirteen acres, to a height of 480 feet— half the height, almost, of the Empire State Building. It is built of some 2,300,000 blocks of stone, the majority of which weigh about two and a half tons each. The placement of these stones is such that the tolerance of error has been estimated at less than 1/64 of an inch. Except for the stones of the interior, which were quarried locally, most of these blocks were hewn from the Arabian range of hills a good many miles to the east, dragged down to the Nile, loaded onto rafts, conveyed across the river, then dragged inland to their present site. The priests who, centuries after its erection, transmitted the tradition of the pyramid's building to Herodotus may have been close to the mark: the construction, they told him, lasted ten years, engaging the labor of 100,000 men, who were relieved by fresh crews every three months For the pyramid bears a hieroglyphic inscription which records that the quantity of onion, radishes and garlic consumed by the laborers added to an expenditure of 1,600 talents of silver. The

Dr. Herbert C. Brichto is Professor of Bible.

imagination is strained by the effort to visualize the tens of thousands of peasants who toiled to produce the food for this work-force, the gangs of water-carriers who trudged the sands to slake the thirst of the hewers and stone-dressers who sweated under the merciless African sun. How many were felled by sunstroke, how many lives were snuffed out, how many bones crushed when a human draft-animal lost his footing, when a roller slipped, the sand shifted, a boulder toppled. And all this for what? To provide a tomb for the cadaver of one man—a pharaoh of Egypt.

To the modern mind this herculean labor suggests a further line of surmise. How many in the work-force were slaves, how many over-seers plied the lash, how many soldiers were required to suppress the populace groaning under the caprice of so cruel and vainglorious a tyrant? Was such the nature of the servitude endured by the Israelites in Egypt? But questions such as these are wide of the mark. For the biblical account makes it clear that the Hebrews who served the pharaoh were as reluctant to respond to Moses' call to freedom as the pharaoh was loathe to release them. And once in the arid wilder-ness, the Israelites were quick to propose a return to the fleshpots of the delta, yearning already for those very radishes, onions, and leeks listed on the pyramid. In the sense of being chattel the Israelites were not slaves at all. They maintained their family units and tribal auto-nomy, continued in possession of their considerable flocks, and the royal grant of the best grazing lands was never rescinded. Indeed, the *nogeśim,* the foremen of the Israelite work-gang, were themselves Israelite tribesmen. The work performed by the Israelites did not, in all likelihood, differ essentially from the corvée labor willingly per-formed for the ruler by the native population of Egypt.

The key word is "willingly," just as the key symbol of ancient Egypt is the pyramid. All the evidence points to one conclusion: the rearing of the pyramids was an expression of religious devotion and gratitude on the part of the Egyptian populace at large, comparable to the faith and piety which produced the monumental churches and cathedrals of Christendom. The pyramid unquestionably is a tomb—the sepulcher not of a man but of a god. The range of human problems was divided by the rabbis under two headings: relations between man and man, and relations between man and the divine. The ancient Egyptians resolved the problems in both these categories in a monolithic solution. "God is in Heaven, all's well with the world" invites the retort that Heaven is remote and the world is a mess. The Egyptians regarded themselves as earth's most favored people. Protected on all sides by natural barriers of sea, sands and mountains, inhabiting a valley whose fertility was assured by the Nile's regular overflow while other lands suffered drought and famine, Egypt was serene in the knowledge that both the natural and the political order were guaranteed by the presence of the god-king on earth: the pharaoh, who knew the service due to his divine counterparts on high and might even threaten them when cajolery failed; whose deputies administered the justice which proceeded from his mouth; who willed abundant inundations of the Nile, corn to grow so that none went hungry; who assured victory to his armies and (in the words of Henri Frankfort) "whose immense power was deemed capable of sweeping later generations safely into the Beyond . . . [providing] the protection and guidance of their lord even in the dubious regions of the Hereafter." No wonder then that in the whole of Egypt's long history there is no evidence of a single popular uprising.

Ancient Egypt represents history's most absolute monolithic tyranny. For what slavery can compare to the slavishness of those who love their master! And the Bible pronounces its verdict. Egypt must ever be shunned. It is the "house of bondage"—not because Israel was in servitude there—but because where a king is god all men are slaves. It is the "iron furnace"—in our term, the pressure cooker—where all men, natives and foreigners, for all the prosperity they may enjoy, are reduced to the status of property—property of the king, god-incarnate.

The eastern arc of the Fertile Crescent presents us with a theology and a polity which are in striking contrast to the system which ensured the static unity of Egypt. Although the history of this area testifies to successive waves of migration and conquest by various racial or ethnic strains (non-Semitic Sumerians, Hurrians, Hittites, and Kassites; Semitic Babylonians, Assyrians, Amorites, and Arameans), there is a continuity of cultural complex which justifies our speaking of a Mesopotamian religio-political tradition. Except for a relatively few exceptions in a circumscribed period, which have been duly noted by scholars, rulers in Mesopotamia made no claim to divinity. Quite to the contrary, the rulers—while claiming their authority derives from the gods—pride themselves on their human accomplishments in conformity with the will of, and by dint of the help they receive from, their divine patrons.

In contrast to Egypt, where all truth and justice derived from the mouth of the god-king on earth, and where from the plethora of written remains legal formulations are notably absent, Mesopotamian writings abound with many traditions of classic law "codes," contracts, legal precedents, reports of court-procedures, and the like. If the pyramid is the archetypal symbol of Egyptian society, its Mesopotamian analogue is to be discerned in the concept of law, of which the concretized exemplar is the diorite stele which bears the Code of Hammurapi. The pictorial relief on the stele portrays King Hammurapi receiving his credentials from Shamash, the god of justice. The prologue and epilogue disclose that the specific laws derive from the authority of the king; he calls them "my precious words," which he has had inscribed "that the strong may not oppress the weak, that justice be provided for the orphan and the widow." It could hardly be made clearer that the validation of the king's authority, his legitimation as agent of the divine, is and must be demonstrated by the justice which characterizes his rule. This tradition—so familiar to us in the Hebrew Bible—is also blazoned forth in inscriptions in various languages by such rulers as Kilamua of Y'dy-Sam'al, Azitawadda of Adana, Yehawmilk of Byblos. Two features of Hammurapi's stele bear eloquent testimony to this prevailing notion that a king's legitimacy is vindicated by his being the patron-custodian of law and justice. The stele itself must have been erected in the capital city, Babylon, or in one of the other main centers of Hammurapi's hegemony. Yet it was found hundreds of miles away in the Elamite capital, Susa. And—to the chagrin of cuneiform students—an area of the stele was erased and polished as if in preparation for a fresh inscription. In view of Hammurapi's curses invoked on any future king who might deface his stele, erase Hammurapi's name and substitute his own, there can be little doubt that the dread anticipation was fulfilled. An Elamite conqueror chose this trophy, weighing several tons, and had it dragged over hill and dale to symbolize that he, the king of Susa, and no

Babylonian successor of Hammurapi's, was now favored of the gods to exercise hegemony as custodian and administrator of law and justice.

Another glimpse into Mesopotamian royal ideology is afforded by the unearthing of the files of King Ammitakum of Alalakh. Baskets of clay tablets, of which a handful deal with matters of state while several hundred are deeds of indebtedness by citizens of Alalakh to the king. These deeds, spelling out the amount of money lent, the rate of interest, and the penalties for default, led one early student of these tablets to quip: Ammitakum was five percent king and ninety-five percent loan-shark. He thereby missed the overriding significance of these documents. The king was not above the law but subject to it; without legal documents signed, witnessed, and sealed he could no more exact a claim from a subject than the subject could from the king.

The rule of law and constitutional monarchy both have their home in Mesopotamia. Whether in Hittite Anatolia or Assyria or Babylonia, the king—for all his claim to be the earthly deputy of the gods—was not absolute; like the king of the gods in the pantheon above, he was *primus inter pares,* first among equals. While strength of character or his fortunes in war might enhance or diminish the degree of power exercised by a given monarch, every king in Mesopotamia—like his heavenly counterpart—was subject to having his proposals in weighty matters debated and rejected in the *puhrum,* the assembly of nobles, and, in addition, submitted to the colleges of priests and prophets who manipulated the omens or in otherwise fashion served as the oracular channels for the will of the gods.

E. A. Speiser, a noted Semitist and one of the great cultural historians of our day, was so impressed by Mesopotamia's cultural achievements in the establishment of the role of law and of constitutional monarchy, complete with a system of checks and balances, that he wondered if much of substantial significance had been added during the millennia separating that polity from our own. Indeed, he speculated on the ideological dissatisfaction implied in the biblical narrative of God's command to Abram to leave his native Mesopotamia. Relations between man and man, Speiser argued, were so ideally resolved in that socio-political system that the dissatisfaction must have been with the *theological* base of pagan Mesopotamia. The very democratic or parliamentary procedures which worked so satisfactorily on earth were a miscrocosmic reflection of the same procedures operative in the divine macrocosm. But the very aspirations which men find best fulfilled by democracy on earth are frustrated by democracy on high. A polytheistic parliament, where various values, embodied in various deities, constantly clash—where a value wins one day to be defeated the next—provides no stable base for human guidance. In the realm of the divine, man demands a hierarchy of values, a Supreme Dictator who orders them once and for all eternity; in short, the monotheistic thrust.

Turning now to the biblical mind on matters of polity, we find that in common with its neighboring societies to the west and east, biblical Israel shared an abhorrence of chaos, aspiration for order, a sense of an intimate relationship between the structuring principles of the realms of the divine and the human. Hence in the Bible, a grateful appreciation of, and a demand for loyalty to, the institutional conventions which make for order in society. What is striking, however, is that Scripture, which propounds normative regulations for so many aspects of the life of the individual and society, refuses to commit itself in favor of or against any particular form of government Rather it accepts the forms in any given period and subjects each of them to a fine, impartial criticism in terms of its success or failure in achieving God's norms. Patriarchal paterfamilias, tribal senate, charismatic magistrate (*shophet,* wrongly translated as "judge"), hereditary monarchy, priestly theocracy—each and all can supply human governance at its best and at its most despicable.

The patriarch Abraham is portrayed as hospitable sheikh and slave-owning warlord. Jacob wrests future dominance from elder brother Esau/Edom by morally questionable means, in his own family foments sibling rivalry among his sons, and is characterized by his descendant, the prophet Hosea, as more fool than knave. The charismatic Samuel combines in himself the roles of civil magistrate, warleader, priest, and prophet, only to be rejected by the people he led so successfully; while the *shophet* Samson, dedicated from birth to be an abstemious Nazirite, turns out to be an asocial bully-boy, as wily a trickster as he is lustful a womanizer. Town councils can be suborned, clan courts may be bribed, tribal parliaments can urge claims of democracy against impending monarchy while their narrow allegiances leave them easy prey to the enemy without. Kingship is scorned in Jotham's parable as an ambition limited to those whose weakness and unproductivity render them least fit for the office. Yet Israel's national polity reaches its pinnacle of success in the reigns of David and Solomon, the former a usurping upstart, and the latter a tyrant who sows the seeds of tribal discontent, leaving the whirlwind crop of rebellion to be reaped by his son Rehoboam. The prophet Isaiah can denounce his king's entangling alliances and military adventurism, expropriation of the peasantry and failure to provide avenues of legal redress, while remaining to the end a passionate royalist, certain that a heaven on earth will yet be established in Judah by a future prince of the Davidic dynasty. Jeremiah is in principle not opposed to monarchy, nobility, priesthood, or prophetic guild—yet he fulminates against their incumbents as incompetent kings, treacherous nobles, degenerate priests, and prophets of falsehood (in the name of Yahweh).

Let us digress for a moment from the biblical scene to reflect on our own frequently murky concept of democracy. Democracy, we realize, is not a form of government but a quality inhering in some governments. It is an idea or philosophy which underlies, or may underlie, a variety of kinds of government. A republic differs from a monarchy in that the head of state is not a king; but both republics and monarchies may or may not be democracies. The essential element in democracy is the notion that the bodies which have the exercise of government derive their authority and legitimacy from the consent of the governed; and hence, in theory at least, are subject to revocation and replacement. Whether the powers of rule—executive, legislative, and judicial—are vested in a single body or divided between several organs, all governments are oligarchies: effective rule is the province of the few But in a democracy the few are ultimately subject to the many, whose will is expressed in elections, plebiscites, referendums, and yes—in lawful rebellion.

Whether we resort to the canons of pure reason or admit the pragmatics of historical experience, there would seem to be no enterprise more futile—certainly none more melancholic—than that of trying to judge between the claims of autocracy and democracy. Complementary values which do not easily lend themsleves to hierarchical ranking will be pitted against one another by the proponents of one or the other system: cohesion, stability, order, and solidarity on one side; autonomy, liberty, equality, self-determination on the other. Consider how tarnished becomes royalty's halo when a royal pedigree is traced back to the triumph of a robber baron or marauding pirate. How absurd the logic of dynastic succession, which, blind to genetic accident, will with fastidious fairness entrust the scepter to the firstborn of his sire be he genius or cretin! But then consider the absurdities of the pure democracy of Athens decreeing hemlock for Socrates, of cigar-chomping politicos fixing presidental nominations, of democracies where the minority (some ten percent of the population in ancient Athens) tyrannizes the majority, or the majority the minority, or where the majority votes for a dictatorship. And who was the madman who first proclaimed *vox populi vox dei?* Whence the mystic faith that the majority rules by right or rules rightly? Who would be content to have the existence of God determined by a vote in the Irish Diet, Israel's Knesset, or the United States Congress?

This debate, however, is not the subject of our inquiry. Our theme is not defense or critique of democracy, it is the base of Western democracy. And behind that qualification—Western—there lies a stark historic and present reality. Never, not today nor in any past, has more than ten or fifteen percent of humanity lived under regimes which are characterized by the democratic ethos. And that small percentage has been limited geographically to what we call the Western world, parts of Europe and the Western hemisphere. And more significant than the factor of geographical distribution is the cultural, ideational heritage of the populations which have developed and preserved democratic institutions. What I am making bold to suggest is that while the biblical heritage is no guaranty that its heirs will opt for democracy, no people in recent times has sustained democratic principles that is not heir to the biblical tradition. Can this be a matter of sheer coincidence? Possibly. But not, in my opinion, very likely.

Without arguing a cause and effect relationship as between the biblical heritage and the development of democratic institutions, without involving us in the question of whether it is the material substructure which determines the ideational superstructure or vice versa, I am suggesting that the Bible puts forward certain ideas about man and his nature, about God and His attributes, which constitute a logical *sine qua non* for the democratic ideology and for the democratic institutions which that ideology alone can sustain.

Two basic biblical tenets can be stated so simply as to present the appearance of a paradox: the supreme dignity of all human beings, and the basic untrustworthiness of every human being

Let us consider the first, the supreme dignity of all human beings, embodied in man as created in the image of God—not Israelites or Jews, male or female, but—humanity as such constituting one family descended from a single set of parents. The dignity of all men is embodied in these two ideas (divine image and common descent) and in numerous moral inferences drawn from these ideas. No such categorical and absolute propositions are, to my knowledge, to be found in any literature independent of the Bible. Not a statement of equality in capacity, beauty, or talent—but equality in moral dignity: universal entitlement to all rights *qua* human rights. Not surprising, then, the recurrent theme in Scripture: *kagger ka'ezrah,* equal rights for Israelite citizen and alien alike. Or, "You must love the alien as you do our own." This in a world where xenophobia was, more often than not, the rule.

Now to the other principle, the basic untrustworthiness of every human—in theological language, the sinful nature or condition of man. A conclusion drawn not from any *a priori* determination of human nature, but rather from the postulate of man's dignity (the divine image specifically includes endowment with freedom of will), and from an existential reading of man's history, that is to say, man's proclivity for making the wrong choice, failing to accord to his fellow the dignity he claims for himself. Given the chance (and the chance is constantly being given), most men will, nine times out of ten, prove themselves to be stinkers. The good man is one who has a somewhat better batting average.

To these two biblical tenets we may add a third: the continuity, the ubiquity, the universality, of revelation. That is to say, in matters of morality—in questions of right and wrong—every man (and all men) knows in his deepest being which is which, knows because God has imprinted it there. As in Plato's theory of general knowledge—it is all there at birth, and teaching is merely the process of educing from each of us what he already knows—so the biblical concept of moral knowledge. But unlike the Socratic notion that all wrong-doing is out of ignorance, that no one knowingly does wrong, the biblical idea is that man does wrong despite his knowledge that it is wrong. Willfully he stops up his ears, willfully makes his heart a stone.

Hence the biblical ideal of the moral autonomy, the self-govern-ance, of every individual. Hence, too, the corollary that the very need of humans to be governed by others of their species is itself a reflec-tion of human sinfulness. Where brothers should unite for the good of one and all, their anarchic, self-blinded, suicidal selfishness renders them a herd of wild horses running every which way.

When the federated tribes of Israel are being picked off separately by the Philistine enemy, it is the very autonomy of the tribal councils which prevents their putting up a common front. They need a single overlord to force upon them the unity they must have to survive and to which they cannot of themselves agree. They ask for a king, and when the oracle points to Saul, God is pictured as saying, "This fellow will rein in my people/hold them fast in harness." Yet when Samuel is miffed by the call for a king—a reflection on his own leadership capacities—God's answer is: Let them have their king, it is not you whom they are rejecting, it is Me. The call for a human king to compel what the divine King invites—that is the sin. Human governance is a necessary evil—necessitated by that evil in man which leads him to spurn the self-governance of which he is (by divine grant) capable.

It now becomes clear why Scripture can sanction differing forms of government while legislating none. The best and wisest of men may commit the worst of sins. The humblest can achieve wisdom and goodness. Man's role under God is ultimate; no one man or group of men, no one role or office, is ultimate over men. A good king is better than a corrupt Congress. Four hundred prophets may speak falsely while one alone speaks true. A minority may accept martyrdom in the cause of upholding the dignity of all men, a majority may exalt a dictator to demonstrate to itself that it is made up of supermen.

To sum up: Scripture no more legislates democracy than it does monarchy or imperium. Scriptural teaching does not necessarily eventuate in democracy. But without its teachings, democracy can only be a short-lived whim. If man is an accident, all values are nonsense. If all men do not share an equal moral dignity, rights will be determined by might. If moral discrimination is not accessible to all, why turn to the majority for consent? If the masses are asses, why not abdicate government to the best (the meaning of "aristocracy") —say, Plato's philosopher-kings, or perhaps Harvard University professors, or—better yet—God's ministers: pastors, priests, and rabbis!

The argument is capable of further development and demonstration, but it will rest here to allow for a word about the record and the prospects. The record, we must grant (in keeping with scriptural pessimism), is dismal. The most sanguine formulation remains that attributed to Winston Churchill: Democracy is the worst form of government ever devised—except for all the other forms which have so far been tried.

In these United States our own experiment with the democratic impulse has, in this generation, somehow survived racism and republican imperialism, McCarthyism and Watergate, alliances with Diem and Thieu, accommodations with Francisco Franco and juntas in Greece and Peru, Chile and Brazil. Grounds, perhaps, for hope that we may survive detente with the Soviets and *apertura* to Red China. In an age when India's millions will worship a successful politician (domestic or foreign) as a demigod, when China's hundreds of millions can find all truth and guidance in Mao's little book, when newly liberated African peoples can replace colonial masters with such as Kwame Nkrumah the Osagyefo (Redeemer) or that exquisite Ugandan moralist, Idi Amin, when concentrated power is yet deified as ever before—we witnessed the process whereby one man, whose finger on a button might well have written finis to the human adventure, was brought low because he showed himself to be—a liar. Ability has, rightfully and inevitably, a high order of priority in any society. In a democracy it can yield pride of place to character .

The prospects for democracy in the world at large may be as

favorable (or unfavorable) as the prospects for mankind in general. And perhaps vice versa. The prospects for democracy in the West are probably yoked to the prospects for the endurance of the biblical or, if you will, the Judeo-Christian tradition. It is conceivable that the scriptural ideational base for democracy (as we have discerned it), incorporated in the centuries-old collective superego of Western society, may even survive in a kind of civil or secular religion, divorced from the rest of Scripture's theological propositions. That has yet to be demonstrated. For the present, the development of our theme would point to the following as perhaps our most pressing and immediate lesson: the application to ourselves of the biblical insight in the matter of human moral unreliability; the recognition that democracy's weaknesses reflect our human weaknesses; the reflection that moral preaching is addressed first to oneself; that gratitude for our own imperfect democratic institutions dictates a concentration on improving what we have—rather than a prideful (and probably futile) effort to export to other societies a system for which they do not yet own the ideological base, a base cherished and nurtured over many generations.

Scripture is not pollyannish. It does not guarantee human salvation, it provides a basis for hope. Great as is the gap between the ideal and the real, Scripture affirms that the ideal is metaphysically real and may be translated into existential reality.

All that is required is faith; faith in that possibility which is also our most cherished hope. How supreme, then, the irony that faith is lacking—not only in a second-hand revelation when a prophet heralds a dread doom, but also when the inner ear reverberates with God's call and promise. In such a situation modesty and humility, consciousness of one's own weakness and fallibility, are vices not virtues. When Moses (in Exodus 3) stands before the glorious vision of the burning bush, hears of his election to lead Israel into the future, he asks, "Who am I to go to Pharaoh, to deliver Israel from Egypt?" God answers, "It is I Am [*EHYEH,* a name of God] who will be with you." And, as if in answer to Moses' unspoken doubt as to whose voice he is hearing, "And this is the sign that it is I who am commissioning you: When you will have delivered the people from Egypt, you [plural] will worship divinity on this very mountain." To reinforce faith in a promised future, a sign is required in the present. What mockery is a sign which itself lies in the future, which will—indeed—coincide with the promised event! Just so, says Scripture: In the realm of the ideal as in the realm of the real, the proof of the pudding is in the eating.

Reform Judaism:
The Shock of Freedom

ALVIN J. REINES

The ultimate challenge to human freedom is the condition of finity. In its essential nature, the condition of human finity is that the person is not a self-sufficient *causa sui*. He does not possess of himself, within the limits of his own being, the power either to maintain his life or attain meaningful existence. The human person cannot live without air, or survive without water, food, and shelter. He is born and nurtured through interpersonal relations, and without such relations, even beyond the evident dependence of childhood, life has little meaning. Consequently, if the human person is to exist, or exist in a meaningful state, he must act to acquire sustenance and relationship from outside himself. Hence the ability of the person to be free, to determine his own actions, is conditioned by a basic need for things and other persons. The human person cannot do just anything; being finite, in need of the external world, he must act so that the external world responds to and satisfies the deficiencies of his condition.

If it were the case that humans always willed voluntarily those actions that bring from the external world the physical and psychic necessaries they require, the condition of finity would not limit their freedom. Experience teaches us that reality is otherwise. Often a

Dr. Alvin J. Reines is Professor of Jewish Philosophy.

person will wish to pursue one course of action, but discover that should he choose to do so, he would lose from the external world that which he needs to receive. Finity is, therefore, an ever-present threat to human freedom. The dependence upon the external world finity generates leads to the most profound internal conflicts, between the desire of the human to choose as he wishes and determine his own actions, and the desire to meet the terms laid down by the external world for it to satisfy the needs of his existence. When the conflict is resolved by surrender to the demands of the external world, the challenge of finity has been successful, and human freedom has been defeated.

The conflict between the human desires to be free and yet to satisfy the needs of finity is a pervasive theme of the Jewish religious enterprise. For traditional Jewish systems, the classic and authoritative formulation of this conflict appears in the Pentateuch, in the history of humanity that it presents from the Garden of Eden to the revelation at Mount Sinai.

In the beginning, the Pentateuch states, there existed a deity who was not only possessed of infinite existence, but also of the power to give existence and life to other beings. Accordingly, the deity, whose name is given as Yahveh, created the heavens, earth, and all living creatures. Among the creatures was Adam, the archetype and future progenitor of the human species. As described by Scripture, Adam was created finite. His finity generated needs of two general kinds, for other finites, and for the infinite. Adam required among finites, things, such as water and food, and persons, such as the woman, with whom to enter into relationship. Of the infinite, Adam required the power to overcome death. Adam was created structurally destined for annihilation, and nothing in the word of finites could keep him from the death for which he was predetermined. The creator God, Yahveh, Scripture says, provided Adam with all that his finite condition required for life and meaning. Yahveh placed Adam in the Garden of Eden, where water and food abounded; He gave him the woman, Eve, with whom to enter into relationship; and He granted him the ultimate gift, life without death.

And the god Yahveh planted a garden eastward, in Eden; and there He put the man whom He had formed. And out of the ground made the god Yahveh to grow every tree that is pleasant to the sight, and good for food; the tree of life also in the midst of the garden, and the tree of the knowledge of good and evil. And a river went out of Eden to water the garden; . . . And the god Yahveh took the man, and put him into the garden of Eden to dress it and to keep it. . . .

And the god Yahveh said: "It is not good that the man should be alone; I will make him a help meet for him." . . . And the god Yahveh caused a deep sleep to fall upon the man, and he slept; and He took one of his ribs, and closed up the place with flesh instead thereof. And the rib, which the god Yahveh had taken from the man, made He a woman, and brought her unto the man.[1]

Deity did not satisfy the needs of Adam and Eve generated by their finite condition without demanding that a price be paid. Adam and Eve must surrender the freedom to do as they wish. In the Garden of Eden are two trees from which they are commanded not to eat under pain of death.

And the god Yahveh commanded the man, saying: "Of every tree of the garden thou mayest freely eat; but of the tree of the knowledge of good and evil, thou shalt not eat of it; for in the day that thou eatest thereof thou shalt surely die." [2]

Finity has taken from Adam and Eve the right of self-determination. They cannot have both the freedom to do as they wish and the perfect security that comes from divine providence in overcoming the limits of finity.

In time, Scripture states, a conflict between the desires for freedom and security develops within them. Despite the satisfaction of their needs by the Garden of Eden and Yahveh's care, Adam and Eve want the freedom to act as they wish. In face of the terrible punishment of which they have been warned, they choose freedom, and disobey the command of deity not to eat of the tree of knowledge.

And when the woman saw that the tree was good for food, and that it was a delight to the eyes, and that the tree was to be desired to make one wise, she took of the fruit thereof, and did eat; and she gave also unto her husband with her, and he did eat.[3]

Yahveh responds swiftly and severely to Adam's and Eve's acts of freedom. He withdraws the special providence they had received which gave them complete protection from the vulnerabilities of their finite condition. Travail, uncertainty, failure, pain, and death now enter human experience. No longer would water, food, and a completely sheltering environment be specially and unfailingly provided the humans. Adam will have to toil in an indifferent, uncertain, and frequently hostile world for what he receives. Eve is condemned to subservience to her husband. She will be the one to bear children, in pain. Finally, the ultimate fate of finity is decreed. Adam and Eve, having been created from the finite, "dust," will now pursue their natural end, to die and return to the dust.

Unto the woman He said: "I will greatly multiply thy pain and thy travail; in pain thou shalt bring forth children; and thy desire shall be to thy husband, and he shall rule over thee."
And unto Adam He said: "Because thou hast hearkened unto the voice of thy wife, and hast eaten of the tree, of which I commanded thee, saying: Thou shalt not eat of it; cursed is the ground for thy sake; in toil shalt thou eat of it all the days of thy life. . . . In the sweat of thy face shalt thou eat bread, till thou return unto the ground; for out of it wast thou taken; for dust thou art, and unto dust shalt thou return."[4]

Moreover, to insure that Adam and Eve do not thwart the decree of death, they are exiled from the Garden of Eden. For in Eden grows the tree of life, which bestows immortality upon those who eat of it. Lest the humans, therefore, through another act of freedom, eat of the tree and thereby acquire infinite existence independent of the power and wishes of deity, Yahveh decrees that Adam and Eve are to be expelled from the garden and never again allowed to return.

And the god Yahveh said: "Behold, the man is become as one of us, to know good and evil; and now, lest he put forth his hand, and take also of the tree of life, and eat, and live for ever." Therefore the god Yahveh sent him forth from the garden of Eden, to till the ground from whence he was taken. So He drove out the man; and He placed at the east of the garden of Eden the cherubim, and the flaming sword which turned every way, to keep the way to the tree of life.[5]

Following their expulsion from the Garden of Eden, Adam and Eve procreate, and begin thereby the subsequent generations of the human species. Every human is born finite, left to cope with the vicissitudes of a neutral and often unfriendly world, without the special providence of the creator God. One person does appear, according to Scripture, who receives an extraordinary measure of divine care. This is Noah, who is saved from the cataclysm of the flood that deity brings to punish humankind for its wickedness. After Noah, however, special providence is again withdrawn from humankind, although deity promises never again to inflict another global catastrophe such as the flood.[6]

It is with Abraham and his descendants, the Israelites, the Pentateuch asserts, that special providence again enters history to assist humans with their finite condition. Two steps primarily mark the return of special providence: a covenant made by Yahveh with Abraham; and the expanded restatement of this covenant in a revelation to Moses and the Israelites at Mount Sinai. The covenant with Abraham is made after a sudden revelation by Yahveh in which he establishes a relation with Abraham. In essence, the covenant states that Yahveh will be the god of Abraham and his descendants, the Israelites, if they will be his people. As god of Abraham and the Israelites, Yahveh will exercise special providence over them to enable them to cope successfully with their finite condition; and as Yahveh's people, they have an absolute obligation to obey his commands.

And I will establish My covenant between Me and thee and thy seed after thee throughout their generations for an everlasting covenant, to be a God unto thee and to thy seed after thee. . . . And as for thee, thou shalt keep My covenant, thou, and thy seed after thee throughout their generations.[7]

At Mount Sinai, the Israelites under the leadership of Moses reaffirm the covenant with Yahveh. Immediately prior to the Sinaitic revelation, the obligation of the people to obey Yahveh is emphasized. Yahveh will provide his special care only if his commands are obeyed.

And Moses went up unto God, and Yahveh called unto him out of the mountain saying: "Thus shalt thou say to the house of Jacob, and tell the children of Israel: Ye have seen what I did unto the Egyptians, and how I bore you on eagles' wings, and brought you unto Myself. Now therefore, if ye will hearken unto My voice indeed, and keep My covenant, then ye shall be Mine own treasure from among all peoples; for all the earth is Mine." . . . And Moses came and called for the elders of the people, and set before them all these words which Yahveh commanded him.[8]

It is of critical importance to understand clearly what the commands of Yahveh are that the Israelites must obey in order to keep the covenant and obtain special providence. The point might first be stressed what they are not. They are not vague, general suggestions that a person do good as the heart prompts. On the contrary, Yahveh's commands are particular, precise, and pervasive rules that control human life in all its spheres of activity. They dictate the beliefs that must be held, the rituals that must be observed, and the morals that must be practiced.[9] Thus the covenant into which the Israelites enter with Yahveh is essentially similar to the agreement implicit in the relation that existed between Yahveh and Adam. Special providence is granted the human person to enable him to overcome his finite condition, but only if the person surrenders his freedom. In the words of the Israelites, the human must affirm: "All that Yahveh hath spoken we will do."

In essence, then, Sinai is Eden regained. The journey of humankind had gone full cycle, from Eden to exile and back again. The special providence that was withdrawn with the exile of Adam and Eve from the garden is now attainable by those who keep the covenant made at Sinai. In return for surrendering their freedom and for obedience to Yahveh, the faithful are protected from the indifference and harshness of the ordinary world. The similarity between the condition of Adam and Eve in the Garden of Eden and that of the Israelites who obey the commands of the Sinaitic covenant is seen in the description of the environment that the latter will enjoy. The world of the faithful is as responsive as was Eden to the needs of the finite person.

And it shall come to pass, because ye hearken to these ordinances, and keep, and do them, that Yahveh thy God shall keep with thee the covenant and the mercy which He swore unto thy fathers, and He will love thee, and bless thee, and multiply thee; He will also bless the fruit of thy body and the fruit of thy land, thy corn and thy wine and thine oil, the increase of thy kine and the young of thy flock, in the land which He swore unto thy fathers to give thee. Thou shalt be blessed above all peoples; there shall not be male or female barren among you, or among your cattle. And Yahveh will take away from thee all sickness.[10]

And thou shalt keep the commandments of Yahveh thy God, to walk in His ways, and to fear Him. For Yahveh thy God bringeth thee into a good land, a land of brooks of water, of fountains and depths, springing forth in valleys and hills; a land of wheat and barley, and vines and fig-trees and pomegranates; a land of olive-trees and honey; a land wherein thou shalt eat bread without scarceness, thou shalt not lack anything in it; a land whose stones are iron, and out of whose hills thou mayest dig brass. And thou shalt eat and be satisfied, and bless Yahveh thy God for the good land which He hath given thee.[11]

Therefore shall ye keep all the commandments which I command thee on this day, that ye may be strong, and go in and possess the land, whither ye go over to possess it; and that ye may prolong your days upon the land, which Yahveh swore unto your fathers to give unto them and to their seed, a land flowing with milk and honey.
For the land, whither thou goest in to possess it, is not as the land of Egypt, from whence ye came out, where thou didst sow thy seed, and didst water it with thy foot, as a garden of herbs; but the land, whither ye go over to possess it, is a land of hills and valleys, and drinketh water as the rain of heaven cometh down; a land which Yahveh thy God careth for; the eyes of Yahveh thy God are always upon it, from the beginning of the year even unto the end of the year.[12]

Still the condition of the Israelites after Sinai, even if they should keep the covenant, is not identical in one essential characteristic to that of Adam and Eve in the Garden of Eden. The Pentateuch says nothing of restoring to humans the life without death that Adam and Eve enjoyed in the garden, and we may reasonably conclude that the utlimate consequence of the finite condition, death, was not removed by Sinai. This conclusion is disagreed with by talmudic and rabbinic Judaism, which maintain that a "world-to-come," or afterlife of perfect peace and meaning, is promised in the Pentateuch.[13] Regardless of the merit of this view, it invites an interesting observation. The "world-to-come" in talmudic and rabbinic literature, and in general usage as well, has the alternative name of Garden of Eden (*Gan'-eden*).[14] For talmudic and rabbinic Judaism, then, the history of humankind turns full cycle in every detail. The person who observes the Sinaitic covenant literally returns to the condition of fully secure existence that Adam and Eve enjoyed in the pristine innocence of the first days of creation.

Analyzing the pentateuchal view of the history of humankind from Eden to Sinai, two states of human existence can be distinguished, one of which may be termed *autarchy,* the other *heterarchy.* In the state of autarchy, the human person's stance is that he possesses ultimate authority over himself, and the consequent freedom to believe and act as he wishes, according to truths and values he himself determines. In the heterarchic state, the person's stance is that some other entity (or entities) possesses utlimate authority over him, with the consequent right to determine the person's beliefs and actions for him. Adam and Eve, when content and obedient in Eden, accepting Yahveh's ultimate authority over them, existed in a heterarchic state. After their exile from Eden, Adam and Eve, living without the commands and guidance of deity, and necessarily, therefore, exercising ultimate authority over themselves, may be taken to exemplify existence in an autarchic state.

The pentateuchal view clearly is that autarchy and true security are opposites. Human persons cannot both live in an autarchic state and enjoy a meaningfully secure existence. The reason, acccording to the Pentateuch, is that humans are finite beings, and finites cannot attain secure existence either through their own powers or those of other finites, whether persons or things. True security can come only from the infinite, from the perfect providence of the creator God,

Yahveh. Since Yahveh will not bestow such providential care unless humans first surrender to him their freedom, as was the case with Adam and Eve, Scripture maintains that secure existence can be attained only by a person existing in a state of heterarchy, in which the right to self-determination has been transferred to deity.

The pentateuchal view that humans cannot at the same time be autarchic and enjoy a meaningfully secure existence is widespread. Consideration of the characteristics of the autarchic state explains why this is the case. Human finity entails limited mental powers, in the person's ability to apprehend truth as well as values. This limitation places the stamp of fallibility and doubt upon all human knowledge, intellectual and moral. Consequently, no human can of himself know for sure whether the object of his belief is real or the action he takes is right. He cannot know with certainty what the future will bring, or whether his morality will prove to be immorality. Yet the autarchic person, limited though his knowledge is, must ultimately base his life decisions upon that which he personally judges reality and goodness to be. To surrender such ultimate determination to any other entity is to abandon freedom and the autarchic state. The insecurity of finite existence that must base ultimate decisions and actions regarding its destiny upon fallible and uncertain knowledge is evident. In a heterarchic relation with an infinite deity, however, such insecurity is dispelled by the conviction that the knowledge and commands upon which life's decisions are based come from a perfect divine mind and are infallible.

Autarchy further breeds insecurity for humans because it demands aloneness. To act in freedom and take ultimate responsibility for decisions regarding truth and values requires a separation of self from all other beings. Decisions that are ultimately one's own must come from thoughts and feelings drawn from the depths of isolated personal being. To a finite being, vulnerable to inquiry and subject to death, aloneness, psychic or physical, is inherently a threat to its existence.

To the human person, accordingly, the state of autarchy is an awesome one. For a finite being, limited in knowledge and power of existence, it is a fearful challenge to live with the aloneness of ultimate responsibility for self. The quality of autarchy is even more vivid when viewed alongside the heterarchy of life in the Garden of Eden or with the covenant of Sinai. The uncertainty of self-authority is contrasted to the certainty of divine authority; the insecurity of finite human existence is contrasted to the security of existence with the infinite deity. For the person who has lived in a state of heterarchy, the terror of a journey to autarchy is sharply portrayed in the expulsion of Adam and Eve from Eden. Their journey beyond Eden confronts Adam and Eve with the life of autarchy and the shock of freedom. It is this shock of freedom and challenge of autarchy that Reform Judaism presents to the modern Jew and the modern age.

The reason why Reform Judaism requires autarchy of its adherents becomes clear upon considering the conditions necessary for heterarchy. In the state of autarchy, the human person is himself his own authority and the ultimate source of his beliefs, desires, feelings, and actions. This is not to say that a person in the autarchic state cannot and does not seek information and advice from others, rather that the autarchic person retains ultimate authority over himself, and makes the final decisions regarding what he will think and do. In a heterarchic state, however, the person surrenders ultimate authority over himself to some external entity that then has the right to command the person what he is to believe, desire, feel, and do. Needless to say, for a person to surrender his freedom to an authority that commands him what to think and do, such an authority and its commands must exist. Simply because persons may desire hetararchic existence does not mean they can have heterarchic existence. They must live in a world that provides the authority and commands necessary for authentic heterarchy, and it is this world that Reform Judaism has destroyed.

To see a world in which authentic heterarchic existence is possible, we need only look to Sinai. In the Sinaitic world, as we have seen, there is an infinite deity, Yahveh, who, the Pentateuch states, has made a covenant with the Israelites. He promises the Israelites special providential care in return for their obedience to his commands. These commands were explicitly revealed to the Israelites, according to the Pentateuch, which represents itself as the infallible source of these same divine commands until the present day. One may then, if he accepts the pentateuchal portrayal of a Sinaitic world, live in a heterarchic state, by following, in unconditional dependence and obedience, the commands of the deity Yahveh. To accept Sinai, however, and surrender one's freedom of self-determination to the Pentateuch, it is necessary to trust the Pentateuch's absolute infallibility. From the viewpoint of Reform, though, such trust is not possible. The reason is that Reform Judaism rejects, and of logical necessity must reject,[15] the infallibility of the Pentateuch. More simply put, in Reform Judaism there is no way to know what is true or not true in the Pentateuch. As the Pentateuch presents itself, judged critically and scientifically,[16] it is certainly not true, and no test exists to determine what in it is true, if anything. The individual Reform Jew must make this decision for himself. As is evident, once ultimate decision-making is required of the individual, he is thrown, of necessity, into a state of autarchy, regardless of whether he wishes it or not. In the following passage, taken from the Pittsburgh Platform of the Central Conference of American Rabbis, the exercise of autarchic freedom in Reform is demonstrated. The Pentateuch does not determine what is valid in Reform Judaism, rather, Reform Jews determine for themselves what is valid in the Pentateuch.

We hold that the modern discoveries of scientific researches in the domain of nature and history are not antagonistic to the doctrines of Judaism, the Bible reflecting the primitive ideas of its own age, and at times clothing its conception of Divine Providence and Justice dealing with man in miraculous narratives. We recognize in the Mosaic legislation a system of training the Jewish people for its mission during its national life in Palestine, and today we accept as binding only its moral laws, and maintain only such ceremonies as elevate and sanctify our lives, but reject all such as are not adapted to the views and habits of modern civilization.

We hold that all such Mosaic and rabbinical laws as regulate diet, priestly purity, and dress originated in ages and under the influence of ideas entirely foreign to our present mental and spiritual state. They fail to impress the modern Jew with a spirit of priestly holiness; their observance in our days is apt rather to obstruct than to further modern spiritual elevation.[17]

The central importance in Reform Judaism of the state of autarchy, in which humans possess the freedom of self-determination, requires a new evaluation of autarchy in religious life. Historically, the Jewish religious enterprise, in common with Western religions generally, has been bitterly opposed to autarchy and the view that freedom is a fundamental privilege of humankind. The position has been that a claim by the finite person to the ultimate right of autarchy is sinful hubris, and rebellion against the creator God. Certainly, the Pentateuch, and Scriptures generally, Jewish and Christian, present this view. As great as the opposition of the Western religious tradition has been to autarchy, so in equal measure has it been partial to the state of heterarchy. Heterarchy, the Western religious tradition maintains, in which the human person surrenders his freedom to deity, is the only moral position. Moreover, the Western tradition holds, heterarchy is the only state through which the finite person can attain soteria,[18] intrinsically meaningful existence. This view of Western religion, that autarchy is immoral and irreconcilable with soteria, is not based upon experience but prejudice, which may be termed the heterarchic prejudice. The heterarchic prejudice is incompatible with Reform Judaism, and in general, with the religious outlook of many persons in the contemporary world.

The heterarchic prejudice pervades Scriptures. In the Pentateuch, the stories of Adam and Eve in the Garden of Eden, and of the Israelites' covenant made with Yahveh at Sinai, epitomize the heterarchic point of view. In both narratives, obedience to an authority other than oneself, the deity Yahveh, is accounted the highest good, and rewarded; whereas acts of freedom and self-determination are regarded as rebellion, and punished. The following passage from Numbers, in which the Israelites are commanded to wear fringes, amply illustrates the heterarchic prejudice. The reason given for the fringes is that they will serve as a constant reminder to the Israelites that they should always obey the commands of Yahveh, and forgo autarchy and their own free choices.

And Yahveh spoke unto Moses, saying: "Speak unto the children of Israel, and bid them that they make them throughout their generations fringes in the corners of their garments, and that they put with the fringe of each corner a thread of blue. And it shall be unto you for a fringe, that ye may look upon it, and remember all the commandments of Yahveh, and do them; and that ye go not about after your own heart and your own eyes, after which ye use to go astray." [19]

Through the ages, untold anguish and difficulties have resulted from the heterarchic prejudice. Yet it is a viewpoint that in the light of our earlier discussion can well evoke sympathetic understanding. The finite condition of the human person, which renders his existence vulnerable and uncertain, produces in him anxiety and other negative moods that threaten to empty his life of meaning. Since the dawn of history, many persons have believed that a heterarchic relation with an infinite deity is the only way to overcome the negations of finite existence, the only path to soteria. Thus autarchy, with its freedom and aloneness, is, they fear, a threat to soteria, and as such to be condemned. It is this view of soteria, I believe, that gives rise to the heterarchic prejudice of Scriptures and of the Jewish religious enterprise, which has historically based itself upon them.

As Reform Judaism shows, however, humankind is entering into a different age, with a new religious consciousness. The heterarchic prejudice is now obsolete. Despite the shock of autarchic freedom to the human bounded by the limits of finity, it can no longer be maintained that autarchy and soteria are mutually exclusive. New insights into the human inner world, and new knowledge of the outer, make it clear that autarchy and soteria are indeed reconcilable.[20] Still, there is much to be done to bring the autarchic way to soteria into our religious communities. Ridding ourselves of the heterarchic prejudice is only a first step. Until this step is taken, however, we will not even have begun the great journey that lies before us.

NOTES

1. Genesis 2:8–10a, 15, 18, 21 f.
2. Genesis 2:16 f.
3. Genesis 3:6.
4. Genesis 3:16, 17, 19.
5. Genesis 3:22–24.
6. Genesis 8:21 f.
7. Genesis 17:7, 9.
8. Exodus 19:3–5, 7 f.
9. Examples of the explicit nature of Yahveh's commands as contained in the Pentateuch extend from the dogmatic requirement of believing Yahveh is god to the prohibition of work on the Sabbath and the interdiction of adultery and homosexuality. The penalties prescribed by the covenant for disobeying Yahveh's commands, which is what constitutes a violation of the covenant, are often severe. For example, the penalty for disobeying the aforementioned commands is death.
10. Deuteronomy 7:12–15a.
11. Deuteronomy 8:6–10.
12. Deuteronomy 11:8–12.
13. Sanhedrin 10:1.
14. See, e.g., Pesaḥim 54a and Nedarim 39b.
15. See "Authority in Reform Judaism" in my *Elements in a Philosophy of Reform Judaism* (Cincinnati, 1976).
16. The critical method is the procedure employed in Reform Jewish scholarship to interpret the Bible.
17. Declaration of Principles, the Pittsburgh Conference, 1885.
18. Soteria is broader in meaning than usually connoted by "salvation" (Hebrew ישועה), referring to a state that can be produced naturally as well as super-naturally.
19. Numbers 15:37–39.
20. This position will be elaborated upon in a forthcoming work that is now in progress. See generally my *Elements in a Philosophy of Reform Judaism*.

Sustaining Ourselves as Jews: An Educational Blueprint

SYLVAN D. SCHWARTZMAN

Recently I heard an intriguing definition of an optimist and a pessimist. An optimist says, "This is the best of all possible worlds." The pessimist agrees.

I suspect this holds true for the prevailing views about Reform Jewish education, generally focused on the religious school. A broad look at the innovations, the experimentation reported by numerous congregational bulletins, by publications of the Union of American Hebrew Congregations, the *Pedagogic Reporter,* and other journals, tends to promote a favorable impression.

Add to this the increasing emphasis on relevance in Jewish studies and the growing move toward more individual instruction and experience, as well as the introduction of a wide variety of newer teaching tools, described in *Midstream* as far back as December 1972 by Walter Ackerman in "The Present Moment in Jewish Education." Among these are the expanded use of multimedia and extensive community contact, the open classroom, contract learning, programmed learning, scheduling modules, mini-courses, sociodramas, day-long and weekend retreats, shul-ins, and many more. From this one could well derive a real sense of well-being and optimism.

Dr. Sylvan D. Schwartzman is Professor of Jewish Religious Education.

"All this may be so," replies the pessimist, but as Harold S. Himmelfarb, Assistant Professor at Ohio State, recently put it in *Analysis* (September 1975), things are certainly far from being rosy. In fact the title of his study, "Jewish Education for Naught," aptly conveys his conclusions. The very Jewish children we educate, he tells us, are really culturally deprived—culturally deprived, that is, in terms of knowledge, identification, and involvement as Jews. His conviction is plainly that Jewish education in this generation is generally a failure, and in terms of their potential advantages, Jewish children among all the ethnic groups are the most seriously deprived. A gloomy assessment indeed!

Well, who is right? The optimist or the pessimist? One is here reminded of the rabbi who was doing some counseling with a couple having marital difficulties. The rebbitzin, out of curiosity, was eavesdropping from the other room.

First the rabbi turned to the husband to listen to his version of the situation. When he had concluded with his long tale of woe, the rabbi responded, "It sounds to me as if you are right."

"Just a minute!" exclaimed the wife. "You haven't heard my side of the story," and she began to pour out all her complaints. The rabbi listened patiently till she had finished. Then to her the rabbi said, "On second thought I believe *you* are right."

The rebbitzin couldn't contain herself. She burst into the room and shouted at her husband, "How can you possibly say that both of them are right?" To which he calmly replied, "You, too, my dear, are also right."

To be sure, looking at Reform Jewish education from the perspective of a century one does observe many pluses. For instance, we have only to compare our present texts with those few of a hundred years ago, drab and uninteresting. Contrast the facilities learners enjoy today over against the dark basements in which our great-grandfathers endured their Jewish studies. Consider the expansion in terms of the length of one's formal religious education which ranges now from nursery school through high school and even into college. On every hand we find experimentation in curriculum, new emphasis on teacher training, the growth of the camping movement, and a phenomenal explosion of adult education. From all this one could surely conclude that Reform Jewish education is rapidly moving ahead in the right direction.

Against this, however, there are certain facts that just cannot be disregarded. Too much contemporary evidence makes us painfully aware of shortcomings. Ties of Jewishness have grown weaker, as have people's senses of Jewish identification and their religious convictions. What Leonard Fein said in 1972 in *Reform Is a Verb* seems increasingly true. There is indeed a "high uncertainty as to what it is that being Jewish really implies, involves and demands," and most of our people haven't the foggiest notion of the answers. This is being exposed all the more today in terms of rapid Jewish acculturation and assimilation, a sharply rising rate of intermarriage, a growing loss of interest in things Jewish, and even an open revolt against fundamental Jewish values.

Again we stand athwart optimism and pessimism. Nonetheless, both optimists and pessimists seem to share certain common presuppositions for sustaining ourselves as Jews. And from the vantage point of a hundred years of Reform Jewish life as embodied in the Centennial of the College, they deserve to be enumerated.

Stating them succinctly, we observe, first of all, the clear assumption in the whole process of Reform Jewish education that, come what may, we are determined to preserve ourselves as Jews. Otherwise, why all the effort, why all the expenditure of funds, the investment of energy, in our educational venture?

Secondly, we are committed to a meaningful Jewish existence in America. Else why the need for the development here of a Reform movement, for all the Reform educational material and a liturgy in English, for the existence of a Hebrew Union College to train American rabbis?

Thirdly, we are convinced that the Jew can indeed bridge the gap between the two worlds in which he lives, the world of modern knowledge as it exists in this last quarter of the twentieth century and the world of historic Judaism as it has developed over nearly four thousand years. In a very real sense this College reflects a healthy synthesis of the two through its scientific approach to Judaism.

Fourthly, we believe that Diaspora Jewish existence, which insures the non-isolation of Jews, is indispensable to the continuation of both

Jewish and human existence. Recent Jewish experience has proven Reform historically right in affirming this position. For, realistically, despite the glorious heroism of our brethren in Israel, how long would that State have survived without a vital American Jewry to come to its aid politically and economically? And to what extent is it possible any longer for Jews in a self-imposed ghetto to help determine the fate of mankind in this age of potential universal holocaust? Surely we American Jews sense a renewed mission of even greater consequence in the fact that we live in an atomic age in which the future of the whole human race will depend upon decisions made largely in Washington, and with this an imperative of even greater import than the mission proclaimed by Isaiah. The world will certainly not be spared by Jews who choose to isolate themselves in Meah Sh'arim or Williamsburg.

Fifthly, in the century ahead survival will be significant only for those Jews who, successfully bridging their two cultures, fathom the meaning of their continued existence in terms of a *God*-given mission. This theological emphasis in religious education must predominate in what has inevitably remained the essence of the Reform Jew's very being.

Finally, if such be our goals, then everything else we do pedagogically is simply a means to these ends. Our concern with relevance, pupil interest and innovation, or even the transmission of Jewish knowledge per se, important as all of these may be, is subsidiary to the objective of producing a Reform Jew. And if there is no longer a definition of what a Reform Jew is or what he/she ought to be, then our whole program of religious education becomes an exericse in futility.

To summarize, it is the very character of Reform Judaism itself, as it has developed in the past hundred years and as it seeks to move into the century ahead, that will determine the perimeters and contours for the educational process that will sustain us as Jews here in America.

To this end we need to be much more specific in what we are attempting to do. If we were building a structure of any kind, the very first question we would ask is, what is its function? To produce an office building we would certainly not prepare plans for a garage. To build a home is not to use some blueprint intended for a department store. Here is where we need to be absolutely clear. What is it we are seeking to build? Or putting it another way, what kind of Jewish education expresses our unique character as Reform Jews?

Review what we have agreed upon as our fundamental assumptions. Our form of Jewish education must be directed to the preservation of Reform Jews who understand and are committed to their responsibilities as Jews in a vastly different world from that of the shtetl. It predicates itself upon a meaningful Jewish existence in America, not a vicarious reflection of what transpires elsewhere, even in Israel. It serves to bridge the contemporary scene with long historical Jewish experience. It recognizes the critical as well as the divine mission of the American Jew for the survival of all mankind.

The development of this kind of Jew is the business of Reform Jewish education. Let there be no mistake about it! The means we adopt in the promotion of Reform religious education, no matter how appealing, must contribute to these ends. A program of values-clarification which begins with the assumption that there is no such thing as right or wrong has no validity for Reform Jewish instruction. Some of its methodology, to be sure, may be useful for technique. But without the conviction that Judaism holds certain basic values, a Jewish education is pointless.

If much of Reform Jewish education today seems confused and jerry-built, the reason is clear. That blueprint so essential for congruity and cohesion in the Reform educational enterprise has somehow been lost for want of an understanding of its premises and the inherent relationship that must exist between these and the program it maintains.

Little wonder, then, that camp experience often bears virtually no relationship to the basic learning that is generated within the religious school, or that religious school curricula are irrelevant to what presently prevails in Reform homes. Even many adult educational programs seem unrelated. Aren't we, moreover, paying far too heavy a price—much more than we can afford—by encouraging each congregation to do "its own thing" educationally? The time has come for us to encourage a bit more of a sense of unity of purpose in Reform Jewish education, without, however, insisting upon uniformity. We need to establish that kind of instructional blueprint which starts with goals, and then proceeds to implement them through adherence to four basic elements.

The first two involve the principle of "polinearity." In one respect, polinearity represents a concept of Reform education that requires multiform and multilevel learning. It recognizes that different educational approaches and programs are necessary for different groups of people. Just as Judaism cannot be monolithic but offers a variety of paths to God, among them worship, study, *gemilut chasadim* and *tzadaka,* holiday observances, celebrational experiences as Jews, and the like, so Reform Jewish education is multiform. It consists of the different tracks for learning that are required by the different kinds of individuals who make up our educational constituency. Often groups of the same age are at vastly different levels. Individuals also have varying concerns and temperaments that seriously influence the nature of the educational process.

A seventh grade, for example, or a class of adults, might well split up into a number of subgroups, all of which will be involved in Jewish learning but in widely different ways. Some individuals might be deeply concerned with study for its own sake—actually we do have a sizable number of people who are interested in learning as an end in itself. Others might be spending their time gathering wider Jewish experience locally, nationally, and even internationally by jetting over to Israel to find out about the realities of Jewish life there. Another segment could be studying life-centered problems as Jews. Others might be devoting themselves to rendering particular service, such as preparing a Seder for non-Jews or programming for a particular institution, as, for instance, a Jewish home for the aged. There are also limitless possibilities for Jewish learning through creative projects; e.g., filling in a number of the gaps in current Reform Jewish thought, producing new forms of Jewish music and worship, developing a popular literature of Jewish values for different age-levels, and even producing a volume on Jewish family guidance, a Jewish "Dr. Spock," if you will. And imagine the possibilities for a group concerned with religious-centered experience, learners in pursuit of the Numinous, trying to discover God's presence in scientific discovery, through exploring the cosmos, human relations, comparative religion, and the like!

Here, then, is one meaning of polinearity—multiform education in line with the Jewish concerns that individuals have, all of which are thoroughly legitimate. We have here a symphony of Reform Jewish learning, each aspect of which complements the other.

The Reform congregation thus is a community of individuals involved in a wide variety of learning experiences. Here not only children, but adults, parents, and grandparents, are variously involved in the educational process. And the resultant learning contributes to each individual's fulfillment as a Reform Jew.

But polinearity has a further and equally vital dimension. An effective Reform Jewish educational structure must have living experience for its base. By itself formal education alone is never really adequate, and it is high time that we recognize this as fact. We who know the research of Jean Piaget have no question that learning results from the interaction of the individual with the environment. And the hard data confirm the truth that most religious training, when divorced from the environment, has little lasting effect. This is Howard Himmelfarb's conclusion about Jewish education generally, and it simply confirms what we have gained from earlier intensive studies of Catholic education. For in *Education of Catholic Americans,* Greely and Rossi made it very clear that Catholic schools have a lasting impact only on those children who come from staunchly observant Catholic homes.

The blueprint for an effective Reform Jewish education thus requires an indigenous climate, commencing with the very birth of the child. It demands a Jewish environment supplied by both parents and grandparents throughout the child's early years and beyond, and the reinforcement of Jewish playmates who can share their common Jewish experiences, talk together in Jewish terms, sing Jewish songs and dance to them, amuse themselves with Jewish games, and enjoy imaginative Jewish play. Long overdue in America are such things as a Jewish Disney World and a whole panoply of exiting recordings, video cassettes, games, and even crib objects which begin shaping the Reform Jewish personality at the youngest possible level.

We must also recognize the urgent contemporary need to develop the extended family; that is, a kinship of individuals not necessarily based upon an actual *mishpacha* of blood relationship. Rather we conceive here of small groups which, by sharing common interests and concerns, dedicate themselves to mutual Jewish sustenance.

Such new configurations are already starting to appear in Reform circles with the establishment of *chavurot,* through the development of family camping, through closer involvement of foster-grandparents, as well as actual grandparents, with the nuclear family. And many of these elders themselves have to be trained in order to learn how to carry out their Jewish roles with their grandchildren.

In the process, I suspect, we are going to have to reassess the operation of many of today's congregations. Some may no longer be able to function as they once did. They may have to become umbrella synagogues that shelter a series of *chavurot* or groups of like-minded individuals who live together in high-rise apartments or in particular neighborhoods.

We are also going to have to reappraise the character of the Jewish community. To what extent do its institutions and organizations provide a pervasive Jewish climate? What is it, for instance, that differentiates a Jewish home for the Reform aged from a similar non-sectarian institution? What kind of crafts will the residents produce? What sort of educational programs will it carry on? What kind of social events? Religious activities? What really makes the institution distinctively Jewish?

Similarly, how does a Jewish family-service agency make manifest its particularly Jewish historical sense of concern for Jews and transmit Jewish values in an explicit fashion? In what way is a Jewish hospital really Jewish? To what degree does a Jewish community center, a Federation or a Welfare Fund, and a whole host of agencies yet to be established, contribute demonstratively to Jewish life?

Beyond this, there are other special needs that must be met. Where are our Jewish needlepoint projects, our Jewish craft shops, our community libraries of Jewish recordings and books, our museums of Judaica, our own universities for Jewish religious study? Where are the patrons who support the Jewish arts on a level not unlike that which they do municipal symphonies, museums, theaters, and the like, so that they encourage Jewish creativity in that Golden Age which beckons us become in reality the greatest Jewish community in the entire history of our people?

In this connection I would remind you of the comments of one of the notable physicists of our time, a man whom many rank in his own right with Einstein as one of the truly "greats" of this age. His name? Isador Isaac Rabi, the distinguished professor emeritus of physics at Columbia University and a Nobel laureate. Recently he was asked by the *New Yorker* to describe the particular influences in his life that most vitally affected his career. And his response was to point to his home life where as a youngster the Bible was constantly read to him in Hebrew and Yiddish. "A profound experience that I had," he said, "revolved around the first verses of the Book of Genesis. They were very moving to me as a kid. The whole idea of the creation—the mystery and philosophy of it. It sank in on me, and it's something I still feel."

Yes, polinearity in the first instance demands multiform, continuing education at every level from birth to death. But it also requires a rich experience that thoroughly immerses the individual in a Jewish environment created through design and not by chance. And the most evident need of Jewish life in this second century lies exactly here. Consequently it is the educator, rather than the fund-raiser, who must determine the priorities for Jewish continuity; that is, if a meaningful American Jewish existence is the objective, and if in the long term, as in the case of Rabi, the whole world is to benefit from the dynamic of a Judaism of consequence.

There are, briefly, two other indispensable features of our educational blueprint, both interrelated and patently obvious. One is an insistence upon realistic, delimited educational objectives. And with this we must also engender a sense of optimism in what we are about.

Too often, in the past, Reform Jewish education has promised far more than it could ever hope to fulfill. One has only to reread "The Guiding Principles of the Commission on Jewish Education," prepared by Dr. Solomon Freehof as a preface to the "Union Curriculum" of 1970, to understand the impossibility of ever attaining the movement's professed educational objectives. All that such an overwhelming set of demands produced among rabbis, educators, and learners alike, was a universal sense of despair.

If this century has had any meaning at all for us, let us hope that it has at least convinced us to accept more realistic aims for Reform Jewish education, aims that can be achieved in measured stages and which provide the learner with a continuing sense of success.

This, in turn, promotes educational optimism, an optimism that naturally encourages still greater effort on the part of teachers and learners alike. It is not unlike the principle of *mitzvah goreret mitzvah,* attesting to the truth that every worthwhile achievement, small as it may be, succeeds in producing still more. The alternative is to reinforce a feeling of failure which inevitably breeds futility and pessimism. We need always remind ourselves that Mount Everest was never conquered without establishing a series of base camps all along the way. Nor did a single climber ever start out for the summit with less than wholehearted confidence.

So much, then, for our blueprint—polinearity in terms of both the educational approach and an environment offering a vivid, living Jewish experience, coupled with realistic, delimited objectives capable of being realized, and developing, in turn, a high sense of confidence in the results.

But a sobering word of caution. Thus far that blueprint for sustaining ourselves as Jews exists only on paper; nothing more. To convert it to reality requires an enormous investment. This Isaac Mayer Wise soon discovered when he had to close Zion College here in Cincinnati (most likely) a year after it opened. It was only two decades later, in 1875, that his blueprint for a viable American rabbinical seminary had the necessary support to assure the continuity of this Hebrew Union College, now truly world-renowned. But do you know what it has cost over the past century to sustain this school? A minimum of one hundred million dollars, plus the indomitable labor and love of countless tens of thousands of dedicated Reform men and women of Cincinnati, from all over America, and in fact, the entire world.

As we commemorate this Centennial, and facing a whole series of urgent priorities, will we be equal to the coming century's demands for sustaining ourselves as Jews? To what degree are we determined to convert our educational blueprint for today into reality? That question can only be answered by each Reform Jew, but I would hope that the response would be something like that given nearly a half-century ago when George S. Counts, the noted educator from Columbia University, spoke in a similar vein about the pressing needs of American education in his day.

It was Counts who, in the very depths of the Great Depression, put the future directly in the hands of a similar audience of men and women with the following challenge: "Do we really wish to be on the cutting edge of change?" he asked them. "Do we really? Then," said he, "let me tell you my answer. My answer is yes." Pausing briefly, he then asked his audience, "What now is *your* answer?"

This is basically the same question we face as Reform Jews in contemplating our own educational future, and what, pray tell, will be *our* answer? Do we really want to be on the cutting edge of change as we move forward into this second century of Reform opportunity? What say we? Is our answer, too, a resounding yes?

Temples Then and Temples Now

DAVID B. WEISBERG

For many of us, it is hard to think back a decade or two and recall with precision the sequence of events that happened to us in the past. How much more difficult, then, is it to thrust our minds back, not decades or even centuries, but millennia, all the way back three thousand years to the ancient world of people, things, and ideas that existed at the time when the Hebrew people lived in their land and were composing what we now know as the Bible. Paradoxically, it is possible now, in the last half of the twentieth century, to say more about antiquity than any preceding generation, all the way back to the time of the events we shall discuss this evening. The reason for this is that more than one hundred years of discovery and explora- tion in Bible lands have given us fresh material, straight from the sources, with which to judge the people who lived then. The very titles of the books published give a sense of the excitement of discovery and the thrill of deciphering. *The Dawn of the Gods; History Begins at Sumer; They Wrote on Clay; New Light on the Most Ancient East; The Greatness That Was Babylon; Deities and Dolphins.* I think

Dr. David B. Weisberg is Professor of Bible and Semitic Languages and Associate Editor of the *Hebrew Union College Annual.*

one of the reasons it is important to know what happened in the past is that human events repeat themselves, and those who are fortunate enough to have studied the past, no matter how remote, are probably going to be in a better position to understand modern events as they unfold. For example, a knowledge of the strategic problems of petty powers in the ancient Orient gives one profound perception into the maneuverings of the descendants of those powers today.

But there is more to it than that. It is hard to be uninterested when we think of cultures that flourished so long ago. We are naturally curious as to what these ancients were thinking, how they lived their lives. We want to know what their law said, what poems inspired them, what their family life was like, how they earned their livings, and what was their religious worship. Sometime ago, when I was lecturing at the College of Jewish Studies in Chicago, a woman asked me one of the most perceptive and important questions I have ever heard. This question has remained with me all through the years since. Her question was, "Were the people of ancient times any different from us? Have we changed at all in the course of three thousand years?" Of course, this woman was well aware of the fact that much in human life has changed. But what has changed is the technological circumstances of life. What she wanted to know was, has the essential human being changed at all? Has human character developed to any degree in the three thousand years that have passed? Do we find people today more ethical, more moral, less likely to hurt their fellowmen, less likely to believe in magic or superstition? From the question of this woman comes the title of my lecture, "Temples Then and Temples Now."

What I would like to do with you this evening is to explore the religious cultures of the biblical world—I should say, some of them—to see how, if at all, the religious perceptions of ancient people differ from our own. My plan is to take you back into the past with me to observe three religious phenomena. These religious phenomena are: first, a look at the activities that went on in a temple on a typical day in ancient Mesopotamia, including the care and feeding of the statues that the ancients worshipped; second, the reading of a selection from an ancient hymn from a prayer book from ancient Babylon; third, a celebration of the New Year's Festival as it took place in the ancient

Orient. What I would like you to do, while we are examining these points, is to keep in mind the following questions. Are there any significant points of contrast or comparison with our own religious observances, and is it possible to detect any phenomena that would point to the evolution of ideas or sensitivities from that day to this? Can we see at all that our ideas are more advanced than those of ancient people?

Let us first imagine the activities of an ancient temple on a typical day. The hour is dawn, the sun has not yet risen. A figure, clad only in a specially designed skirt, is making his way out into the temple courtyard. He has just been in the inner sanctum of the temple, offering special prayers and chants before the god and goddess of the city. Now he is awaiting the rising of a special group of stars sacred to Babylon. He eagerly scans the horizon, trying to pick out the constellation. At last he sees it and greets the appearance of the stars with a melodic chant, culminating in the recitation of a magic incantation. The stars are sacred to Babylon, and the priest whom we are watching is reciting a prayer that has been passed down from father to son for millennia. The origins are obscured in the mists of time. He pauses for a moment when his prayers are completed. Then he notices that people are astir in the courtyard of the temple; the sun is rising and people are beginning to bustle about their daily tasks in the sacred precincts.

At one side of the temple courtyard we see a pen for sheep and cattle. Some of these animals will be used for the daily sacrifices that are offered in the temple to the patron deity, the spouse of the deity, and minor members of the divine entourage. This entourage consists of a family of gods which mirror, in a way, the family of the king of the city. There are official temple shepherds and cowherds whose job it is to supervise the movements of the temple animals, care for the flocks, and see that the sacred meals are supplied with meat from the animals of the god.

Hidden away in another corner of the courtyard, we see part of a building complex within the temple walls. This building is the temple foundry, a place where precious metals, like gold and silver, are assayed, smelted into ingots for precious jewelry for the image of the deity. The source for this gold and silver is a wicker box, called by the ancients *qūpu,* which, some of you might recall, is cognate with the Hebrew *qupāh* or *arannu,* which is cognate with the Hebrew *'arōn.* The box is placed by the entranceway to the temple, and pious worshippers, filing in past the gate, deposit their precious trinkets as donations to the temple. Within the inner area of the temple, not visible to us or accessible to the common man, is the temple bank and armory. In the bank the ingots, jewelry, and gems are stored. Money is loaned out to those wishing to take a loan—the usual rate of interest being 20 percent per annum.

However, let us imagine that this morning a special messenger comes into the temple precincts. He bears a letter from a man whose name is Nabu-šum-ukīn. Nabu-šum-ukīn has been kidnapped by outlaws some seventy-five miles from his home in a nearby mountain range. The letter asks that the temple ransom him from the outlaws and thereby allow him to return to his city. It was the law of the land in ancient Babylon that the temple was obliged to ransom such citizens and aid in their return to their families. One of the temple's officials goes into the bank and withdraws the sum of fifty shekels of silver, the ransom demanded by the captors. The money moves under guard to the outskirts of the city. It is eventually delivered to the brigands, and Nabu-šum-ukīn is reunited with his family after a harrowing few weeks in captivity.

As we continue to observe the movements of people in the temple on the typical day, we notice ten soldiers filing in military formation past the gate toward the rear of the temple complex. These soldiers are headed for the temple armory. Their unit is being outfitted for a military expedition to the Mediterranean. They need to receive bows, arrows, daggers, a special leather garment to be worn around the chest that serves as a kind of personal body armor, and metal helmets. All of these objects are manufactured, repaired, and stored right here in the temple precinct, where they are disbursed not only to soldiers in the national army, but to the local militia, who serve as watchmen and police for the city in which the temple is found. The soldiers receive their weapons and armor, and the record of disbursements is duly made and deposited in the house of records. Let us imagine for a moment that we are in the house of records, or archives, also located on the temple grounds. In this library are stored thousands of documents, among them receipts for loans, records of sale of real estate, slaves, agricultural commodities, lists of offerings, records of adoption, and countless other types of administrative records. The clay tablets upon which the records are written are stored, one upon the other, on specially constructed shelves. At the edge of these tablets are briefly noted summaries of the transactions so that the clerks working in the archive building will be able to see at a glance what the records are, in case reference is made to them and they are needed. The script used in this writing is called cuneiform script, after the Latin word *cuneus,* which means "wedge." The writing is called "wedge-shaped" because of the tiny incised wedges that make up the six hundred-odd signs of the syllabary. The people living and working in this temple have not yet used the far more convenient mode of writing that employs alphabetic characters.

So far we have just observed the multifarious economic activities going on in the temple courtyard. But is there no place where actual religious worship is carried on in this typical day from antiquity? Yes there is, but this activity goes on in the sacred confines of the temple's inner sanctum and is never visited, seen, or known about by the simple man in the street. Permission to enter these sacred grounds is restricted to a special group of administrators and priests known as *ērib bīti,* or "those who are permitted to enter the house." These *ērib bīti* are given special identity cards that enable them to pass by the guards posted at the doorways to the inner sanctum. Some of the people permitted to enter the restricted areas are craftsmen, woodworkers, jewelers, plasterers, painters, and the like, whose job it is to refurbish the cult paraphernalia in need of repair, to repair the walls of the temple, or to create new objects of beauty to be used in the worship of the local deity. Other *ērib bīti* are temple administrators, not themselves priests, whose job it is to oversee the manifold affairs, economic, political, and otherwise, in which the temple is involved. Still other *ērib bīti* are the Babylonian priests who are charged with the task of seeing to it that the ancient rites are performed correctly. In antiquity, there was no premium put on innovation, invention, or novelty. The society was organized around the principle of replication in the traditional manner. What was old was good. What was new was newfangled and suspect. The right way to do things was the way the ancient sages had done them and the way they would always be done until time itself wound down to an end.

Let us put ourselves in a properly awe-stricken mood and imagine that we are granted an interview with the same priest we earlier observed in the temple courtyard. He politely informs us—no offense meant, of course, to the visiting foreign dignitaries—that it is strictly forbidden for non-*ērib bīti* to set foot in the sanctuary. However, in honor of our visit, he is willing to divulge some of the special rites performed in the daily care of the statues of the gods, it being understood that these matters would be prudently kept to ourselves and not divulged to anyone. It is hard for us to understand his excitement and pleasure as he describes how the statues are daily dressed, washed, fed, and taken for walks. The polytheistic relation he is describing, with its manifold deities and their images, is so far removed from us in time and background that we cannot really enter his mindset and appreciate his words. Nevertheless, we do listen politely as he transmits his account to us. He begins by pointing out that rarely, if ever, are Mesopotamian deities portrayed in any but human form. He patiently explains to us that it is not the statue itself that is worshipped, but rather the spirit that inheres in the statue. The god is considered to be present in the image if that image shows certain specific features and is cared for in the proper manner. Most of the images are made of precious wood. Those that are not dressed with garments are plated with gold. They are fashioned with characteristically staring eyes made of precious stones inset in a naturalistic way, crowned with tiaras and adorned with special chestpieces that are suspended from the neck with gold and silver chains. The garments are changed in special ceremonies, in accordance with the ritual requirements. The images themselves were fashioned in special workshops in the temple. They had to undergo an elaborate and highly secret ritual of consecration to transfer the lifeless matter into a receptacle of the divine presence. During ceremonies that took place in the dead of night, the statues were endowed with "life," and eyes and mouth were "opened" so that the images could see and eat and were subject to the washing of the mouth, a ritual that imparts special sanctity.

As the priest speaks to us, a special melody is heard from the sanctuary, and the smell of delicious foods comes to our nostrils. The images are being fed, the priest explains. The gods of this temple, he continues, are offered two meals per day, a larger meal in the morning and a smaller meal in the afternoon. Both meals consist of the same courses, and differ only in the quantity of food for the gods. A table is brought in and set before the image, precious bowls are set before the god, water for washing is offered in a bowl, several drinks are arrayed along the left side of the table in a prescribed arrangement, and containers with beer and other beverages are set out. After this, special cuts of meat are served as the main dish. Finally, fruit is brought in in a specially pleasing arrangement as a dessert. The food brought before the god is not thought to be literally consumed by the statue. Rather, it is waved before the god, perhaps in a manner that is echoed in the biblical *tenufā* or *terumā* ceremonies, and then the meal is served to the king. At the conclusion of the meal, the statue is taken for a walk. It is paraded through the temple precincts. At this point the ordinary worshipper gets his chance to glance at the splendor of the divine image. On occasion, the god even goes for a stroll through the city streets, and on rarer occasions still, goes on a boat trip to a neighboring city up the river. And with this vivid description of the care and feeding of the gods in ancient times, let us bid farewell to this ancient site so that we may continue in our observation of ancient religious customs.

Let us turn our attention now to the subject of ancient prayers and hymns. The people of antiquity, in the matter of their prayers and hymns, were not much different from ourselves. They expressed their deepest hopes as well as their most profound fears by means of the prayers they recited in their own homes and in public worship. Many of these magnificent liturgies, private petitions to the gods or psalms of praise, have survived the ravages of time, and we are now able to study them and gain a new perspective of the inner life of the ancient people. Some of the shortest prayers we have from antiquity come from the names of the people themselves. These names, usually consisting of three parts, frequently contained a pious wish, prayer, or utterance of thanksgiving. Here are a few examples of the prayers enshrined in names, as we may call them. The name of one Babylonian king, Nabonidus, means: "May the god Nabu be honored." The name of another Babylonian king, Nebuchadnezzar, more correctly, Nebuchadrezzar, comes from the Babylonian words *Nabû-kudurri-uṣur*, which mean: "May the god Nabu preserve my boundary stone." The word "boundary stone," of course, is used for "inheritance," and in this context seems to mean "son." Here is a rather picturesque combination, with the name of the chief deity over the Babylonian pantheon, Marduk: Dūru-Ṣēru-Marduk, which means: "Marduk is a mighty wall of protection." Still another name with a familiar pious prayer contains the name of the underworld deity of ancient Mesopotamia, Nergal. Nergal-uballiṭ means: "May Nergal keep well." Other categories of ancient prayers more familiar to us in the West are hymns to the gods, an example of which I shall give briefly below. Prayers on behalf of the king and his family and by the royal family to the god, songs addressed to ancient temples, songs of woe, like the Book of Lamentations in our Bible, and the unique type of prayer, a letter addressed to his deity by a worshipper. It is my personal feeling that these ancient examples of piety and devotion do not fall short of our own psalms and religious poetry, except in the fact that they address polytheistic deities. These psalms may address goddesses and gods and not the God of Israel. However, their poetic diction, meter, loftiness of thought, and lasting beauty are discernible even when viewed through the perspective of three thousand years of history, and are enough to recommend them to us even today. Permit me, then, to recite for you four stanzas of a magnificent hymn to Ishtar, who was the ancient goddess worshipped as the goddess of love and war. The English translation is my own.

Sing of the Goddess, most august of all. Let the lady of mankind, the most exalted of the Igigi (heavenly deities), be praised. Her lips are sweet as honey, her mouth is life. At her appearance we are filled with awe. Glamorous is she, and glory rests upon her head. Her many forms are beauty. Her eyes are clear and bright. Who of all could equal her grandeur? Splendid are her decrees. Ishtar, her grandeur, who can equal it, she is sublime. Splendid are her decrees. She is the Queen of Heaven. The gods harken to her commands. Before her all fall down in worship. Her brilliance dazzles. Female and male, homage to her render.

For our final excursion into the religious life of ancient man, I would like to take you back once more to an ancient city. But this time, let us return to Ur, in Babylonia, one of the main cities of southern Mesopotamia, for a celebration of a New Year's Festival. In very ancient times, that is, four thousand years ago and more, this festival had, as its central feature, a rite of fertility which involved the sexual union of the king of the land and the high priestess of the temple, who represented the goddess of the city. This union was meant to ensure, by magical means, the continuing fertility of the land, abundant crops, a plentiful supply of water, and the fruitfulness of its inhabitants. It was hoped that, just as the union of the king and the priestess signified virility and fecundity, so would those desired qualities be transferred back to the land itself and to all who dwelled therein. The fertility rite took place in the ziqqurat, or temple tower, which was the central feature of many of the temples in ancient Mesopotamia. However, as time went on, it seems that the sacred union between the king and the high priestess no longer occupied the central spot in the cult as it once had done. Gradually, a more modern celebration centered around the personality and mythology of Marduk. As it later developed, the feast took place on the first eleven days of Nisannu, which is the Babylonian pronunciation of what later became Nisan in the Jewish calendar. This month included the spring equinox. On the eve of the fourth day of the celebration, the Babylonian epic of creation was recited. This has an interesting parallel to the fact that Rosh Hashana in the Jewish calendar, while not in the spring festival season, but rather in the fall harvest season, is celebrated at a time close to the recitation of the first few chapters of Genesis, *berešit*. Something is known about the procession during the New Year's Festival from excavations at Babylon itself. The highway passed through a splendid gateway called the Ishtar Gate, whose walls were decorated with glazed enamel bricks on which the figures of bulls and dragons appeared in relief.

Our trip into antiquity is now drawing to a close, but before we conclude, let me remind you again of the two questions I asked you to keep in mind while were were visiting these ancient folk. Are there any significant points of contrast or comparison with our own religious observances, and is it possible to detect any phenomena that would point to the evolution of ideas or sensitivities from that day to this?

In answer to the first question, I must confess to you that I, as well as almost every other scholar interested in the ancient Near East, am always delighted when I can discover a biblical parallel that will cast some light on a practice perhaps otherwise long forgotten. But we should bear in mind that the purpose of studying these ancient societies is not to find parallels; the purpose is to understand these ancients on their own terms, and thereby, hopefully, to better understand ourselves. We have discovered many such points of comparison and have discussed some of them with you this evening. As for points of contrast, I find them to be fewer than I would have imagined when I began my research in this area. The more I study, the more it seems to me that these ancient people were in no way different from ourselves, except in regard to the tools that their culture gave them and the varying social mores of their time. In personal makeup, insofar as this is discernible in the countless documents, personal letters, poems, and the like that have come to light, there is absolutely no difference between us. It follows that there has been no evolution of human psychology, no radical transformation of the individual personality. Even given the massive technologies now at our disposal and the thousands of additional years of civilization that separate us, they had their scientists and we have our magicians, as you can see by opening any newspaper to the column on astrology. Time and again we find peering at us from antiquity those precious lines that tell us about their identity with us. Consider, for example, these marvelous words from an ancient charm recited by a pregnant woman: "May my baby look like my husband. May my baby look like my husband." From those days long ago we see a letter of a son to his parents, a child's toy, a prayer expressing hopes for good health and long life. Things really haven't changed that much, have they?

The Breaking of the Tablets: Pique, Compassion or Iconoclasm

EUGENE MIHALY

My focus is a body of literature created approximately from the first century B.C.E. to the sixth century C.E. The place: ancient Palestine. The languages in which these works were written are Aramaic and Rabbinic Hebrew, with a generous sprinkling of Greek and Latin loan words, and an occasional phrase in Syriac. The total body of writings of which I speak is subsumed under the general heading, Rabbinic Literature. I shall, however, deal with only one aspect of the totality, that part of the literature known as Midrash.

Midrash is a Hebrew word derived from the root *darosh,* a word which appears a number of times in the Bible. Its basic meaning is to seek, to search, to investigate. The prophet Amos hears the Divine Voice admonishing, "Seek ye Me and live." *Dirshuni,* a form of the same root *darosh,* seek, seek ye Me.

The prophets, who spoke with the authority of "Thus said the Lord," searched for reality, for the truth, "the way by which men shall live, not die," by going to the Source, to the Author of the true and the real. The process was a vertical one. The prophet was in direct communication with the Source of being and meaning. In other periods and in

Dr. Eugene Mihaly is Professor of Rabbinic Literature and Homiletics and Executive Dean for Academic Affairs.

different cultures, the truth was to be discovered by consulting, by seeking out the oracle, be it at Delphi or some other sacred spot. Whatever the source of truth was, however, the way to its discovery was to search out, to seek, to investigate, to commune, to be in communication with that source, *Darosh, Lidrosh,* and thereby discover the way, the direction, the imperative, and the truth.

In time, the messages received by outstanding individuals and leaders like a Moses or an Isaiah or a Jeremiah are written down and transmitted. They become authoritative. They are canonized. Their words now assume a sanctity. The ritual demands and the ethical imperatives are now discovered, not by vertical communion, not by the individual's being in immediate touch with the Ultimate Source. The process is now a horizontal one. The truth now resides in the written text. To discover the way, "God's will," one must now turn to Sacred Writ, canonized Scriptures.

The prophet as the authority who has a direct channel to the Source is now displaced by the teacher, the knowledgeable wise man, the expert who has studied sacred, traditional literature. As the accumulated body of sacred literature is progressively canonized and invested with the authority of Scriptures, in the centuries before the Christian era, prophecy as a phenomenon disappears. The school and the synagogue, where the sacred texts are studied under the guidance of a teacher, a rabbi, now take the place of the prophetic circle. Study, searching out, expounding, investigating, exegesis of Sacred Writ, is now considered the most laudable activity. The Ultimate Source is still invoked, but only as an aid in discovering the truth contained in the written word.

With the development of more complex societal structures, urban centers, an authoritative written Constitution, a juridical system and courts of law, there is a natural tendency to minimize the role of, and even mistrust, the ecstatic leader who claims the authority of immediate communion, who has a direct channel to the Source. It is hardly surprising, therefore, to read in early Rabbinic literature that "the Sage, the learned man, the *Ḥakham,* is far preferable to the prophet," or that "With the destruction of the Temple, prophecy was given over only to children and fools." The teacher, the scholar, the rabbi who has thorough command of the Sacred Writings and is expert in expounding them, in searching them out, *Lidrosh,* is enthroned as the authoritative figure and the ideal.

The assumption underlying this expositional, midrashic, this "searching out" activity, which was carried on for centuries in the academies and in the synagogues, was that since the Bible is Divinely revealed, it is the source of all truth and all wisdom. Every letter, every jot, is there by design, carefully arranged by a Divine Intelligence, to teach a significant lesson. Each word is a seventy-faceted gem which sparkles a new and ever more brilliant ray as we turn it, and turn it, again and again.

The many levels of meaning are communicated by way of hints, allusions, mnemonics, by means of intricate cipher codes, through metaphor and allegory. To expound Scripture properly and to discover in it a sure guide for all time and every circumstance, one has to be expert in the methods of exegesis. There thus develops an elaborate system of exposition, hermeneutic rules through which Sacred Writ was to be searched out and expounded.

And we know, of course, that if the method of interpretation is broad enough, one can find almost anything in the text. The text easily becomes a pretext. "Peter's idea of Paul is a better idea of Peter than it is of Paul." If the intent in studying a text is to find proof texts for our pet notions, the result is not exegesis, taking from, but eisegesis, putting into.

The Midrash, an exegetic literature, may thus not tell us too much about the meaning of the original text, the Bible, on which it is based. It is a primary source, however, for the culture and civilization of the centuries when the Midrash was produced. The new wine may be a superior vintage indeed, if we are not misled into judging it by the old bottles and the ancient labels.

Everyone who has dealt with classic texts knows that pure, objective exegesis—recovering the original meaning of a text—is an unattainable ideal. We inevitably bring ourselves and our own context to the exposition of a text. The difference is only one of degree. Despite the age-old admonition, "Do not do to Plato what Plato did not do for himself," we inevitably do just that, and each age, more or less, casts him in its own image.

The curriculum of the academy and of the schools, during the early centuries of this era and for several centuries preceding it, used the Pentateuch, the first five books of the Bible, as the primary text. The students, guided by the expert teacher, the rabbi, studied, searched out, and expounded each book in sequence. The beginning of the Book of Genesis afforded the opportunity to explore the prevailing notions regarding Creation, the then-current cosmology or system of metaphysics, aesthetics, and ethical ideals.

One sage, for example, while conducting a session on the Creation story in the first chapter of Genesis, noted that each day's creation is capped by the phrase, "And God saw that it was good." This repetitive epithet indicates God's affirmation and approval of the creaturely world. Strangely, however, no such Divine approval is given to the creation of the second day. The phrase, "It was good," occurs after the creation of the first day, the third, fourth, fifth, and sixth. It is missing after the second day's creation. The rabbi, therefore, poses the question to the class: "Why is it not said, 'And it was good' after the second day's creation?"

After considerable discussion, the answer is suggested that God could not say "And it was good" after the second day's creation because the word "separation" occurs in the account of that day. The text says, "God separated the waters from the waters." The rabbi therefore draws a lesson: When separation occurs, even though it is necessary and essential for creation, nevertheless, God cannot say, "It was good." How much the more so, when there is separation, dissension, and strife which is destructive and harmful, must God withhold His approval and His blessing.

When a teacher, centuries later, repeated this interpretation to his class, he was quickly interrupted by a strenuous objection from one of the students:

"You say, Rabbi, that wherever the word 'separation' occurs, God cannot say, 'It was good.' But look at the account of the first day's creation! The word 'separation' is used—'and God separated the light from the darkness,' and, nevertheless, the first day's creation is capped by the phrase, 'And it was good.' With all due respect, Rabbi, the biblical text itself indicates that the answer you cite from the Midrash is untenable."

After complimenting the student for his perceptive and acute objection, the rabbi replied in the form of a fable: A piece of iron and a piece of gold were having a discussion in a blacksmith's shop. The bar of gold said to the iron, "You are reputed to be the strongest of metals. Why then are you such a coward?" "Look at me!" the gold admonished, "The smith pounds me, he hammers me, and barely a peep out of me. You never hear me shout or cry or complain. And you, Mr. Iron, as soon as the smith touches you, you make such a racket. You cry and complain—the noise you make disturbs the entire neighborhood. A stiff upper lip would be more appropriate, Mr. Iron."

Barely concealing his chagrin, the iron replied: "Mr. Gold, you may be the most precious of metals, but monetary price has little relationship, apparently, to sensitivity and insight. Consider, Mr. Gold, when the smith hammers you, what implement does he use? An iron hammer, made of a metal that is a stranger to you. When an element which is totally strange and alien causes pain, it doesn't hurt quite as much. One more or less expects it. But look at me! When the smith pounds me, he does so with my own flesh and blood, with my brother, another piece of iron like myself. My friend, that really hurts."

"Now let us consider your objection, my dear student," the rabbi concluded, "in the light of the fable. The separation which occurred on the first day was between light and darkness, two elements naturally opposed to each other. Such separation is a blessing. Essential to the creative act is the ability to distinguish between good and evil, light and darkness, cosmos and chaos. The arduous climb out of primeval slime is doomed unless such separation—separation between light and darkness—is made. Such separation merits the Divine approval: "And God saw that it was good." On the second day, however, the separation was in the same element, water and water, between brother and brother. Such an act of dissension and strife cannot receive Divine assent. Such divisiveness is a curse, not a blessing. Therefore, is the phrase 'it was good' missing from the account of the second day of creation, when water was separated from water."

During a subsequent class session, the teacher probed the verse in the first chapter of Genesis that describes the creation of man on the sixth day: "God said, let us make man in our image and in our likeness." "Since man was not yet created," the teacher challenged his students, "whom did God address when he said, 'Let us make'?"

One student suggested that the expression is the plural of majesty. Another, that God spoke to the angels, who according to rabbinic tradition, had been created on the second or fifth day. The final suggestion is that the verse speaks not of remote origins. It does not refer to the creation of the original Adam. Rather, it is the ongoing and ever-present call addressed to each boy and girl as they are about to be married. The verse charges each bride and groom to fulfill the most exalted of human tasks: "Let us make man!" God pleads with each couple, "Take me as your partner, and together let us create a human being."

To communicate the flavor of this literature, let us join a session of the academy in B'nai B'rak, now a suburb of Tel Aviv. The time is the last decades of the first century C.E. The head of the academy is the renowned Rabbi Akiba, the authority of the age who is reputed to have attracted twenty-four thousand disciples. The session is devoted to an exposition of the nineteenth chapter of Leviticus, the section of the Bible that has come to be known as the Holiness Code. The students, seated on the ground in semicircular rows, listen with rapt attention to this saintly sage as he deduces mounds upon mounds of laws and lessons from every jot of every letter. After a lengthy discourse on the verses "Ye shall be holy, for I, the Lord your God, am holy. Each man shall revere his father and mother and observe my commandments," and on and on through the entire chapter, probing the implications of "You shall not place a stumbling block before the blind," "You shall not seek vengeance," and "You shall not hate your brother in your heart." Rabbi Akiba finally pauses—an anticipatory pause—to prepare his audience for something portentous and of special significance. He bends closer to his audience as if to embrace them and speaks almost in a whisper: "Now we come to the most important verse in Scripture. The verse requires no elaborate exposition or explanation. It speaks for itself. 'You shall love your neighbor like yourself.' This is the greatest principle in the Torah."

One hears the stillness as each student ponders the implications of this heart commandment. The gentle voice of Rabbi Simeon ben Azzai, a colleague of Rabbi Akiba, soon, however, interrupts the revery:

"You know, dear students, of my profound respect and affection for Rabbi Akiba. I hesitate to take issue with this great scholar and teacher, and my cherished colleague. This is, however, one of the rare instances when I must express my disagreement with his interpretation. He told us that the verse 'Love your neighbor like yourself' is the central and most significant principle in the Torah, that this is the principle which should guide man's relation with his fellow man. This greatly disturbs me.

"All of us know people who have an active dislike for themselves, who have a contempt for and even despise themselves. Shall such a person, then, treat his neighbor in the same way? Shall he, then, despise his neighbor? There are some who do not even have a self, who have not yet constituted their own ego integrity. Shall they deny that self to others as well? Shall their neighbors be treated as a tool, a vehicle, as if they had no self? No! This principle, this verse in Leviticus, is too relative; it is too subjective. It does not take account of human foible and aberration. To our deep regret, too many are self-destructive or lack any awareness of self. How can such a person use his relationship to himself as a guide in his relating to others?

"The most important principle, the most significant verse," Rabbi Simeon ben Azzai pleaded, "is found at the beginning of the fifth chapter of the Book of Genesis: 'In the image of God created He man.' If man develops an awareness that he and every other human being bears the image of the Ultimate, that he was created in the *imago dei,* it is impossible, then, to treat and to view either himself or others as an object, a thing, an instrument to be used. The divine image makes each human being an end in himself. This is the objective principle which must govern human relationships. The sure knowledge that human beings bear the image of the Creator guarantees the dignity of every man, the self as well as the other."

Through the centuries, every letter, every word, every verse of Scriptures was expounded, investigated, searched out. The lectures, expositions, and discussions in the academy and in the synagogue were transmitted orally from one generation to another, and preserved in the form of notes taken by individuals. The oral tradition and the notes were finally edited and written down. This voluminous literature is the Midrash.

We are now ready, I hope, to consider a biblical narrative with a view toward illustrating how the text was expounded and transformed by successive generations. I omit the ingenious word-play, the subtle exegesis, the intricate hermeneutics whereby the exegete derives his particular interpretation. These elements, the use of the proof texts, are often the most challenging and poetic aspects of the literature. The basic spirit of the literature can, however, be communicated and appreciated without the technical, linguistic details. The story I have selected is found in the thirty-second chapter of Exodus, the well-known incident of the golden calf and Moses' breaking of the Tablets.

The biblical account is typically laconic. It conceals more than it reveals. You will recall that Moses ascended Mount Sinai to receive the Decalogue. The people became impatient when Moses tarried, and they confronted Aaron, Moses' brother, and said to him, "Come, make for us a god to go before us. As for this fellow Moses, who brought us up from Egypt, we do not know what has become of him." Aaron, according to the Bible, readily responded to the people's request. He cast the gold rings and earrings which the people had brought to him into the image of a bull calf. "This," he said, "is your god, O Israel, who brought you up from Egypt."

When Moses descended from the mountain and saw the bull calf and the dancing, he was angry. "He flung the Tablets down, and they were shattered to pieces at the foot of the mountain." Then Moses took the calf they had made and burnt it. He demanded of Aaron, "What did this people do to you that you should have brought such great guilt upon them?" Aaron responded with the lame excuse that all he did was throw the gold in the fire and out came the bull calf. Moses then again ascends Mount Sinai and receives the second set of Tablets. This, in summary, is the biblical report of the event.

It is clear that in the biblical narrative, the villain of the piece is Aaron. The scriptural account also leaves no doubt about the motive of Moses in shattering the Tablets: when he approached the camp and saw that glittering golden idol, the debauchery and the abandon of his beloved people, his dreams a shambles, he is overcome by an uncontrollable fury. He smashes the Tablets into smithereens.

Later generations, centuries after the biblical account was written and canonized, could not accept the simple, plain, obvious meaning of the biblical story. Aaron had, after almost a millennium of accumulated legend and song, assumed heroic proportions. He was, after all, the brother of Moses; the mouthpiece of the stammering, inarticulate liberator, who, like Moses, stood tall before the mighty Pharaoh, and demanded, "Let my people go!" Furthermore, all the contemporary priests who performed the sacred service in the Temple, who made atonement for and cleansed the people of their sins, the teachers of their children, the preservers and interpreters of the Law, they were all descendants of Aaron, that Aaron whom later generations enthroned as the ideal, the paradigmatic priest, the father and exemplar of all the Aaronide priests to follow.

To reconcile the idealized image of Aaron with the biblical text required some quite elaborate midrashizing, searching out, exegesis. The great sage Hillel, the head of the Sanhedrin in the middle of the first century B.C.E., set the pattern: "Be a descendant of Aaron, loving peace and pursuing it." Another sage notes, "When Moses died only the men mourned him; but when Aaron died, the entire congregation of Israel, men, women, and children, bitterly cried." They had lost their dearest friend.

In the first centuries of this era, and for hundreds of years before it, a different kind of Aaron, an idealized, heroic, saintly Aaron, had to be found in the biblical text. All of rabbinic ingenuity, intricate hermeneutics, is mobilized so that what had come to be the real Aaron in the popular mind should emerge from Scriptures. The rabbis thus discovered, through minute analysis of each word in the narrative, that when Aaron is confronted by the rebellious multitude, he is shocked and mortified. If he refuses their demands, they will kill him. But the saintly Aaron is not concerned for his own life. He is worried about his people. If they murder him, the priest in the sanctuary, they will bring sure destruction upon themselves. So he tries a variety of delaying tactics, desperately hoping that Moses will return and save the situation.

He, therefore, suggests to the multitude, according to the rabbinic sages, that the women bring their precious golden jewels. This will take time, and time is what he must buy to save his children from this most serious of transgressions, the sin of idolatry. "Women are too attached to their jewels to part with them," Aaron reasoned. "They may even refuse, and thereby stop this insanity."

His stratagem, however, failed. Everyone is so caught up in the frenzy that women literally tear their earrings and rings from their ears and fingers. Aaron then tries yet another device. He throws the gold into the fire, hoping that the gold would be consumed and destroyed. But to his amazement, a golden calf emerges. It is a demonic power which frustrates Aaron's designs. In desperation, Aaron calls out, "Tomorrow is a festival unto the Lord." Aaron buys yet a little more time, another day. "And note well," the rabbi urges, "Aaron did not say, 'Tomorrow is a festival to the idol.' He said, 'Tomorrow is a festival to the Lord.' " But it is all in vain. Moses tarries, and Aaron is faced with the inevitable.

Finally, after exhausting all the alternatives, Aaron determines that he will accept the full responsibility for the foul deed. Like every hero, he is willing to give his life, to sacrifice his immortal soul, for the sake of his people. "Let the blame fall on me," Aaron decides, "as long as my beloved flock emerges blameless and is saved."

After centuries of dialogue with the text, the weak, spineless Aaron of the biblical narrative is transformed. He becomes the tragic hero, a savior of Israel.

The problems of the rabbinic exegete are, however, not yet fully resolved. He is also deeply troubled by the role of Moses in the narrative. Why did he break the Tablets? Moses was not your average mortal who is overcome by uncontrollable anger. The dream which impelled his entire career was to bring the Word to Israel. Would a Moses destroy his life's goal in a moment of pique? Did he not, even before he descended from Sinai, plead with God to forgive? "Turn from your anger," Moses prays, "and think better of the evil you intend against your people." In a Prometheus-like gesture, Moses even threatens the good Lord himself: "If you do not forgive this people, erase me from your Book." And a dire threat it was, for without Moses there is little left of the Book.

Why, then, would this faithful shepherd, the peer of the prophets, the giant who cast his shadow on all subsequent generations—why would this rabbi of rabbis dash his most precious dream in a moment of pique and deny to his people the Law which would guide them and be their saving grace throughout the ages? The obvious meaning of the text cannot be its real meaning. It is out of character. It denies everything that tradition had come to attribute to Moses.

"If one knows how to expound the Bible, if we search deeply enough and if our deeds and motives are pure enough," Rabbi Samuel, the son of Naḥman, explained to his students in the academy, "the real and profounder meaning in Scripture may be discovered. We know, dear students, that the Tablets were six cubits long and three cubits wide. As Moses descended the mountain, he grasped the Tablets by the two cubits on top, and the good Lord held on to the two cubits on the bottom, to help Moses carry the inordinately heavy tablets of stone. When Israel committed that infamous deed of making the golden idol, God tried to snatch them back and to wrestle the Tablets from the hands of Moses. Moses struggled with all his might to retain his grasp so that he could fulfill his mission and deliver the Tablets to his people. In the struggle, the two Tablets fell and shattered." Moses, according to this rabbi's reading of the text, did not break the Tablets. He tried to save them. He fought God himself to preserve them. The broken Tablets represented Moses' defeat and God's victory. This is the Moses of tradition: a compassionate, devoted shepherd who dared battle almighty God for the sake of his people.

Another midrashic teacher suggests that Moses broke the Tablets, not in a moment of anger, but as a deliberate act—after calm deliberation. Moses reasoned: "The Ten Commandments were given to Israel in order that they do them—because they promised that they would abide by them. Now that they have made an idol, I must, for their sake, break them." "This is to be compared," the sage continued, "to a king who commissioned his messenger to go and betroth a beautiful woman in the name of the king. When the messenger arrived at the woman's house, he found her in the embrace of another man. The king's messenger was overcome by compassion for this lovely creature. He thought to himself, 'If I give her the certificate of betrothal, she will be a married woman and her amorous acts would cause her death.' He, therefore, took hold of the document and tore it into bits. Similarly, Moses said to himself, 'If I give the Tablets to Israel, I will surely cause their destruction. The second commandment cleary admonishes. "You shall have no other gods before me." ' To extricate himself from this dilemma, Moses grasped the Tablets and broke them."

This is another interpretation which emphasizes the compassion of Moses and his concern for the children of Israel. For their sake he would even shatter the sacred Tablets.

In an academy in northern Galilee in the third century, Rabbi Simon, the son of Lakish, offered yet another interpretation of the event. "There are times," Rabbi Simon said, "when in order to preserve the Torah, one must destroy it. When Moses broke the Tablets, God said to him, 'Thank you, Moses, that you have broken the Tablets.' " Rabbi Simon suggests in his interpretation that the Tablets themselves may become an idol when the recipient is not spiritually ready or attuned. He worships, he deifies the Tablets themselves, rather than obey the commandments inscribed on them. Stone tablets, the scroll, the parchment, the book, become the object of worship. To preserve his message, Moses had to break the Tablets. People who worship a calf of gold will also make a godlet of tablets of stone. The act of Moses was thus one of radical iconoclasm, and God thanked him for it. An event originally described as one of pique is, through the ages, transformed into a deed of love and compassion, and finally into an event of shattering idols—of iconoclasm.

The process of Midrash continues. Whenever a serious, searching student engages Scripture in dialogue, whenever he is inspired by and inevitably inspires the biblical text, he is creating Midrash. The opera *Moses and Aaron* by Arnold Schoenberg is a more recent midrashic interpretation of the biblical passage we have been analyzing. Schoenberg's Moses, who never sings during the entire opera, is the uncompromising, stern prophet who conceives of a God who cannot be seen, cannot be imaged, an inexpressible many-sided idea. Aaron the priest, in contrast, the lyric tenor, makes images, symbols. He communicates with and pleases the people. "The stiff stern rod in Moses' hand becomes the supple serpent in Aaron's hand."

When Moses descends from the mountain, he confronts his brother Aaron: "What have you done with my dream?" And Aaron replies, "And you, Moses, what have you done? You have made an image too. What are the Tablets but an image?" In desperation Moses cries out:

Then I have fashioned an image too, false as an image can be.
Thus I am defeated. Oh word, thou word that fails me.

And in despair Moses shatters the Tablets.

Aaron, according to Schoenberg, confronts Moses with the ultimate dilemma. On the one hand, Moses' God cannot be expressed, symbolized, imaged. He is the pure idea, yet He must somehow be communicated. How else would the wanderers in the desert come to know him? Aaron would make images, attractive, seductive pictures and symbols which appeal to the senses, the play-way to God. But the result of Aaron's method is the killing, chilling idol of gold.

Moses ascends the mountain to claim the eternal words inscribed by the finger of God on the Tablets. These ten words will, he is confident, preserve the idea and keep it pristine. Aaron, however, pins him on the horns of the ultimate dilemma: "Moses, you have also made an idol," Aaron charges. "The Tablets of the Law convey only partiality. The part will be made whole, the finite will become infinite, and that is the heart of idolatry."

Here is the problem in all of its profundity: to communicate one requires images—words are images too; they are timebound. And yet, not to use words is to bear moot witness. How are the people to be taught? How can they know? Moses has no answer. In desperation he shatters the Tablets and cries out:

> Word—thou word that fails me,
> O Wort du Wort das mir fählt.

Schoenberg's modern Midrash is perhaps the profoundest analysis of Moses' anguish—Schoenberg's own anguish.

A viable answer is suggested, perhaps, in a very early rabbinic homily: "Rabbi Joseph taught that the Tablets and the broken Tablets were both placed into the holy ark together. They were of equal sanctity." Tablets are necessary, Rabbi Joseph suggests, but along with them must be carried the broken Tablets. To keep even the Tablets from becoming idols, they must from time to time be shattered and the bits and pieces carried along as a reminder that the Ultimate is beyond any possible human expression or comprehension of Him.